The History of

SHIRLEY OAKS
CHILDREN'S HOME

JAD ADAMS and GERRY COLL

"Motherless children,
if no-one loves you in this world
make a start and love yourself."

Alex Wheatle

Deptford Forum Publishing

LONDON 1999

First published in Great Britain 1999
by Deptford Forum Publishing
441 New Cross Road
London SE14 6TA

ISBN 1 898536 86 4

Set in 10pt New Baskerville
by METALanguage

Printed and bound in Great Britain
by Redwood Books Limited
Trowbridge, Wiltshire

Line and tone illustrations by Gerry Coll

Florence Waters
resident at Shirley Schools, 1914–26

This book is dedicated to all the children
who lived at Shirley Oaks 1903–1983

Remembering

Miss Barbara Heath and Miss Delia Moylan

Dorothy

Jean and Mick Cunvin

Gerry and Mary Oliver, their children

Elizabeth, David, Sarah and her husband Ray

and their children Natalie and Jasmine

Paul, Jenny and Carol, former First Key workers

Maureen

Des and Rowena and their children

Megan, Bethany and Joel

Peter and Paul

Wonderful Dee

Teddy Pendergrass

Rita and Alan

Victoria Laughland, founder of Who Cares? Trust, and Leslie

'Going home' from school, c.1959

Sponsors

The authors wish to acknowledge the interest and support of:

Linda Beeks; Frances Bickerton (relief housemother); Christopher Brewer; Patrick James (Tommy) Fall of Yew Cottage 1954-58; John William Lee; Leonard Davidson (Laburnum); The Franklin family; John Francis Baker; Lilian Irene Smith; Mrs N. C. Hawkins; Anthony (Tony) Bay; William Mason & family; Mrs Kathleen Brickwood SRN; Julia K Partleton (Willow Cottage); June & John Salmon (Aunties & Uncles Scheme, 1961+); Charles W. Price (Resident 1957-65); Alan & Jean Barber; Ian & Sue Coherton; St Mary's RC Church; John Miller & Carol (Briar Cottage); Brenda Burton (Daisy Cottage); Brian Maunder; Rosemary Harris (Sister Pepper); Ian & Trisha Robertson; Mrs Heather Murphy (Donnelly); Carol Shearwood; Sarah Curtis; Rev. Peter K. Mansfield; Frank Ridley (1954-1970); Louis Hamer; Mr & Mrs B. George (former resident/assistant housemother); Alan & Rita Passey; Brendan & Gabriel Joyce; Maureen Kearney; Michael McCarthy; John & Carol Taylor; Paul & Gina Noble; Heather Holden; Pam Hurn; Paul & Alison Robson; Val & Bradley Andrews; Christine & Karl Turner; Michael & Martha Nestor; Gerry & Mary Oliver; Dusty Miller; Doreen Lockyer; Alison Cooper; Dr Peter Green; Antony Amoo; Margaret Chater; Maisie Rice; Mick & Jean Cunvin; Sara & Ray Dunning; Eileen & Tony Fleming; ADM Autos; Judith Clayton; Annie Barrows; Jean Jones; Tony Quinn; Christine Moore; Kevin & Alison Casey; Clement Abrew; Audrey Thomas; Dee Chesterman; Elizabeth Oliver; Daisy Styles; Tony Harris; Dennis Milan; Shirley Oaks Hospital; Croydon Churches Housing Association; St John the Evangelist Church; St Andrews RC Church; Raymond & Floyd Stevenson; Mrs Eileen Davis; Alan Davis; Peter Davis; Our Lady of the Annunciation RC Church; Shafts Clothing; Carmelite Friars; Humming Bird Caribbean Cuisine; Katherine Kent; Robin Adcroft; Ida Adcroft Barker; Jennifer Hierons; Neil Correy; Avion; Kevin Pelman; Maureen & Roger Mortimore; Rev. Michael O'Dea; Sue Goggin; Shirley Methodist Church; Wally Bishop; Ronald & Leslie Austin; Siobhan Crowley; Winifred Elizabeth Tuck (Biggin); Rose Stenning (Bishop); His Honour Bruce Laughland QC; Mick Bishop; A.J. Benedict; William & Eileen Austin; Mick Bishop; Jenny Gordon.

Published with the help of a Heritage Grant from Croydon Council.
For more information contact the Heritage Office, Croydon Clocktower, Katharine Street, Croydon CR9 1ET.

The entrance to Shirley Oaks Children's Home, 1907

Contents

Acknowledgements

Arthur Mott, former duty headmaster at Shirley Primary School, gave assistance on educational matters. Tony Harris and Len Chatterton who gave assistance relating to activities and recreation. Staff of the Metropolitan Record Office gave valuable assistance. The photographs on the following pages are reproduced by kind permission from Southwark Local Studies Library (pages vi, 5, 10, 14, 17, 21, 22, 23, 24, 26, 27, 31, 38, 41, 45). Lambeth Archives and Croydon Local Studies Library gave access to written sources. Alan J Robertson developed photographs in the ownership of Southwark Council. Thanks to Leslie Robinson for supervision in design and planning and Vera Brice. Great appreciation to David Oliver for his assistance on all aspects of the book's marketing and production.

Thanks to Ray Wheeler for writing the foreword, and Kerry of Glen Word Processing for undertaking the initial typesetting. I would like to take this opportunity to thank those people who purchased the original 1993 document that paved the way for this final edition. The contacts made by this manuscript have made it possible to produce this book. We are grateful to Raymond and THK for help with the launch.

Many thanks to Jess Steele and Portia Smith at Deptford Forum Publishing, and to Penny Frith at METALanguage.

Preface

Welcome to this commemorative book on Shirley Oaks Children's Home, which was originally known as Shirley Schools and then Shirley Residential Schools. The story gives us a taste of a bygone age. Having lived and worked in Bermondsey my interest was heightened in the Bermondsey Board of Guardians, who inaugurated the buildings of the Shirley Schools and were responsible for the running of the Home for the first thirty years.

After the closure of the Home, I often heard people say: "I could write a book about this place." This sowed the seed in my mind that someday I would attempt to do this myself.

The completion of this task has ensured a more permanent record of some aspects of life at Shirley. Another reason for chronicling the history of Shirley Oaks is because I want to acknowledge some of the events that shaped the history of this Home. I hope this will also have some value to the readers of this book. It attempts to provide a history of the Children's Home that may also be of interest to local historians and people involved in social work. Teachers and educationalists may find it of use when working with children and young people.

Invariably the people who have contributed to the book are mainly those who, as children, grew up in Shirley. They were not asked to share anything they felt uncomfortable with. It was up to them whether they shared the good, bad or the ugly. The book does not seek to 'romanticise' the Home or claim it was an ideal place to live. It was not! It was a place where children were sent, in some cases against their will. Originally the Home was set up for "orphans, poor children from overcrowded districts of Bermondsey and children of parents, who owing to circumstances were unable to keep them". As the years unfolded, the reasons why children came into care changed. Children were received into care through the courts and some were considered to be in moral danger and in need of protection. Life in Shirley for some children was a very unpleasant experience. Many felt unwanted and neglected, not only by their parents but by the system that was supposed to care and look for them. Some children were kept in ignorance of their civil liberties. Growing up in long term care has had a profound affect on some people's lives. Today we hear from various sources allegations of abuse against children in residential care including physical, psychological and sexual. Some of these accusations may date back many years and are made by people who, as children, lived in the care system. Whilst not negating the seriousness of these accusations this book is a commemoration of Shirley Schools and not about addressing or investigating allegations, nor about judging care policies and practices. In some of the text, forenames only have been used for children, to protect confidentiality.

This book is, a history of the Home, describing life and some activities there and should serve simply as a monument to some of its achievements and failures. I hope that the accounts of children incorporated here also reflect the diverse experiences of those not recorded.

I trust that those who read this book will find it interesting. If you were a resident or a member of staff, you may read with your own special memories and perceptions – you lived there, you worked there. Whatever your reactions, I hope this history will highlight some past events for you, creating a sense of fascination and nostalgia.

Interpretation is included where it seems necessary but, in general, readers must bring their own interpretation of these events. The text includes quotations from the official records of the Home; sections of newspaper reports and recollections of former residents and staff. There is, therefore, no single 'view' presented here, but a composite of different attitudes and perspectives. Sometimes, people who have grown up in long term care cannot see beyond their own suffering but the people whose accounts are included here are not representative of that category.

As well as thanking the many people for their accounts of their upbringing and experiences at Shirley, I wish to thank Jad Adams for editing this publication. Jad and myself worked hard on the research; we have been committed to getting the facts right and offering an accurate record.

I also want to thank all the people who felt able to sponsor this book. In a very real sense, you have contributed not to a part of history, but to local heritage. The planning, design and preparation of this book has been extremely time-consuming, but it has been worthwhile because it helps to dispel some of the myths surrounding this Home and the stigma often felt by children in long term residential care. I hope with the millennium upon us, this book gives a real insight into the last establishment of its kind to be built this century.

Gerry Coll

Foreword

As one with a lifelong interest in Croydon, and particularly Shirley, it is a great privilege to be asked to write the foreword for this chronicle of Shirley Schools. This is not just another local history book, important as that is considering there are few books currently in print on aspects of Shirley's history. It is primarily the story of an institution, a residential school, established nearly a hundred years ago by the Bermondsey Board of Guardians. In their attempt to provide a haven from the social evils of their day the Guardians built the Schools on a 'green-field site', in accordance with the best practices known at the time.

One of the authors grew up in Shirley Schools, so first-hand knowledge ensures that the book has been written from experience. Gerry and Jad have spent long hours searching through the records of the Schools held at the London Metropolitan Archives, Southwark and Lambeth Local Studies Library.

Today institutional care comes in for a great deal of criticism. We live in different times from those of the Guardians of Bermondsey. We hear today so many horror stories concerning children in care and the betrayal of trust by those placed in authority. The Schools were set up in the days of 'child-rescue'. The story of Shirley Schools does not gloss over these events but at the same time does not dwell on the negative. The personal memories speak for themselves and may help former pupils to come to terms with their own individual life-stories.

Whoever reads this book – local Shirley residents, past pupils and staff, educationalists or social workers – will find much of interest. They will find many stories woven together charting the history of the Schools. For the original Guardians, who through their altruistic endeavours wanted to give the children in their care a new start in life, the housemothers, who attempted to provide the security that their children lacked, the teachers, who imparted their knowledge and gave their pupils skills that could take them beyond Shirley, and for people who lived in Shirley who were aware of the community within the gates, Shirley Schools were an important part of life.

It is an absorbing book and I wish it every success.

Raymond Wheeler

Introduction

The Poor Law and Children in Care before 1900

The Poor Law, under which the children's Home at Shirley was administered, dated back to 1834. It established workhouses in which the destitute poor would be kept in conditions worse than the worst they might experience outside the workhouse. The objective was to ensure that only those who really needed help would go there; the administrators of the Poor Law did not want the "idle poor" living in luxury on the rates.

It was recognised that there was a problem with the workhouse child, who could hardly be held responsible for his or her poverty. Left in the workhouse, moreover, these children were felt to develop the bad habits of their elders. Large, barrack-like 'schools' were therefore set up from the late 1840s, in which thousands of children would live together.

School Districts were set up in 1849 by order of the Poor Law Board to administer the schools for these child paupers. In the case of the Home studied here, the authority involved was the South Metropolitan School District, which eventually took children from the parishes of Bermondsey, Rotherhithe, Camberwell, Greenwich, Newington, Woolwich and Stepney.

The school in Brighton Road, Sutton, whence came the children who first populated Shirley Children's Home, was built in 1852-55 and was occupied until 1902.

The Industrial Schools and Reformatory Schools Acts of 1854 and 1857 permitted schools to be set up for children who had offended or were in dormitory schools aimed at 'correcting' crime. Industrial schools aimed to prevent crime by caring for the neglected before they became delinquent, giving them an honest trade at which to earn their living. Clearly this is the origin of the 'industrial training' which will be documented in the school examined here.

For most of the nineteenth century, the Poor Law administrators had to provide for destitute or deserted children, or those whose parents were in the workhouse. They had no responsibility for children living in their own homes, however neglected or abused they might be. Acts of Parliament of 1889 and 1899 gave the Poor Law Guardians the right to assume parental rights in the case of neglect, and the Prevention of Cruelty to Children Act later extended this.

These Acts gave legal backing to the attitude that children must be 'rescued' from the families and conditions which might lead them to a life of vice. Hence the efforts which, it will be seen, were made to keep children from their families and previous habitats, including severely restricting visiting from relatives, and having the institutions built far out of towns.

By the end of the nineteenth century, the Local Government Board, which now had overall responsibility for the administration of the Poor Law, was coming in for increasing criticism of its 'barrack' children's homes, which were really nothing but children's workhouses. A report of the Poor Law Schools Committee of 1896 was against large schools. In 1897 the Local Government Board declared that the School Districts would be abolished and the local Unions must make provision for their own children. Criticisms were well taken, but foundered on the question of which alternative to adopt.

Experiments had been taking place in the private sector in Britain and in France and Germany, to establish more humane homes for pauper children. Dr Barnardo's homes for boys were based on large-scale communal living, but when the same system was tried for girls it was unsuccessful; all discipline broke down. The solution was to adopt an idea pioneered by Thomas Stephenson and have the Barnardo's girls in small groups in cottages with a surrogate couple in charge.

In 1898 the Local Government Board looked at five innovative homes run by voluntary organisations aiming: "to bring up destitute or criminal children in habits of religion and virtue". These included the

Homes for Little Boys at Farningham, Kent; Dr Barnardo's Village Home for Girls, Ilford; and Princess Mary's Village Home, Addlestone. Present in these homes were most, if not all, elements which were later incorporated into the children's homes built at the beginning of the next century. There were children accommodated in smallish groups in cottages, in what was called the "family system"; a house mother for each, with widows chosen for preference "as best calculated to gain the hearts of the children, and to represent the nearest approach to the natural mothers", and training so the children would be able to earn an honest living on departure.

The report of the Local Government Board also mentioned the setting of the Home for Little Boys, that it was "a series of homes, like any pretty country village. The home may be taken for a picturesque group of detached villas with its village church, and other buildings, indicative of active life." This could easily be a description of Shirley at its best.

CHAPTER ONE

The Foundation of the Schools

The Shirley Schools of the St Olave's Union were built on what had been Shirley Lodge Farm. This 72 acre site was situated on the north side of Wickham Road, Shirley, where there was a narrow frontage. To the west was the large mansion known as Shirley Cottage, once owned by the Earls of Eldon.

At the time of the Croydon Enclosure 1800 (the Act of Parliament for the enclosure of the commons and common fields of the ancient Parish of Croydon), Joseph Cooper was in possession of some of the fields belonging to Shirley Lodge Farm (*pictured left*).

John Maberly had acquired Shirley House from John Claxton in 1812, and over the next few years acquired more land surrounding the original Shirley House estate, including in 1824 what was to become Shirley Lodge Farm. Maberly was declared bankrupt in January 1822, and his estate was auctioned in 1824 and 1825 by the Bankruptcy Trustees. Shirley House was sold to Samuel Skinner, but in 1838 was acquired by John Scott, Lord Eldon. Shirley House eventually became the Shirley Park Hotel, but was demolished in 1962 to make way for Trinity School (part of the Whitgift Foundation).

William Stephen Watton of Woodside purchased Shirley Lodge Farm in March 1835, at the same time acquiring a meadow to the south of Wickham Road, opposite the entrance to the Farm. William Stephen Watton died in June 1846, and his estate was left in the hands of Trustees, comprising members of his wife's family that included the

Teevans, also of Woodside and local surgeons.

The 1871 Census Return records that James Nicol was farm bailiff. He and his wife Jane came from Kincardine in Scotland. It is probable that they were employed by Margaret Ballardie, also from Scotland, who was renting the main farmhouse. By 1881 Thomas Goddard was in occupation of Shirley Lodge Farm. Thomas and his wife Ann were to be there for the next 20 years. The Census Return of that year describes Thomas Goddard, then aged 42, as a 'Farmer of 60 acres employing three men and one boy'.

At the beginning of 1898, the Bermondsey Board of Guardians set up a Schools Committee with the express purpose of seeking a suitable site in order to carry through the aim of providing a residential school for the children within their care.

The first meeting of the Schools Committee was held on 26 January 1898, and the members agreed to establish a children's home on the cottage Home principle. Within the first few weeks of that year, members visited the Kensington & Chelsea School District Home at Banstead, Surrey, the Shoreditch Parish Home at Hornchurch, Essex, and the cottage homes of the Bridgend & Cowbridge at Cardiff in Wales.

In February 1898 members of the schools committee visited the Croydon Union homes at Mayday Road, Thornton Heath. These homes made a favourable impression on the committee members. The committee minutes provide a full description. There were six semi-detached cottages, each occupied by 12 children under the charge of a foster mother, but no foster father. The cottages comprised on the ground floor, a dining room, kitchen, bath and lavatory, and store room. On the first floor were three bedrooms, the foster mother's room, a box room and two store cupboards. In addition were a wash-house and WC at the back of each cottage. The children went to the local board school as well as church or chapel. Washing was sent to the workhouse laundry, apart from the small items. The children were taught domestic work, but no trade, as no workshop was provided. The cost for keeping each child was 8s 6d a week.

While these visits took place, the search for a new site proceeded. Sites at Stone near Dartford, Sutton, Epsom Downs, Addlestone and Baldwyn Park near Bexley were considered. The Norbury Park Estate north of Thornton Heath was also on the market for £14,000.

By the end of 1898 the Guardians were no nearer finding a new suitable site for the proposed Home. Committee members had also inspected other homes as far apart as Sheffield and Bath. They were not impressed with the standard of the Camberwell Home at Heaton Road, especially the food: "sausages and potatoes hardly seem sufficient fare for the meal of the week – the one which an ordinary working man's child looks forward to as being better than the ordinary week-day meal."

In July 1899 a letter was received by the Guardians from Mr A. Durbin of Grove Park, drawing to their attention to the Shirley Lodge Farm which had been recently placed on the market. Committee members visited Shirley Lodge Farm on 26 July 1899. It was the best site yet considered and architects Newman & Newman of Tooley Street were instructed to open up negotiations with the vendors, the Trustees of the late William Stephen Watton.

In October 1899, the Local Government Board approved the purchase of the site at a cost of £260 per acre, defrayed by a loan over 50 years. Sketches were submitted and, in March 1900, Newman was asked to submit full working drawings.

The first few months of 1900 were taken up by wrangling over the rental of the site. The Guardians required Thomas Goddard, who occupied Shirley Lodge Farm, to pay £100 rental for the six month period from 25 December 1899 to 24 June 1900, rather than £40 as Goddard had hoped. Goddard visited the Guardians' office and presented his own proposals which were subsequently referred to the Schools Committee. Negotiations became acrimonious, and eventually the Guardians insisted that Thomas Goddard should pay £150 for rental up to 31 October 1900, with hay crop to be removed by the end of July and the remaining arable land cleared by 31st October. If these proposals were not accepted, then Goddard need only pay £40 but must quit by the end of April.

On 5 April 1900 the Guardians received a letter from Fuller, Moon & Fuller, agents acting for Goddard, advising them that Goddard was prepared to give up the farm, there and then and pay the £40. Goddard sold all his livestock, implements and equipment, and gave notice to his farm hands. Henry Hicks, who had been a tenant at a cottage on the farm for 14 years, was allowed to stay on under the same terms as he had held previously with Goddard.

The Schools Committee minutes record that the land was not maintained well, with the hedges and banks neglected for some years. Trespassing from the footpaths across the land was taking place. Notices were placed in the local press inviting tenders for removal of the crop by the end of October. A noticeboard was fixed, giving warning that the Guardians of St Olave's Union would prosecute unauthorised persons found trespassing.

St. Olave's Union.

ACCOMMODATION FOR THE
AGED AND INFIRM POOR

∘ LADYWELL ∘

NEWMAN & NEWMAN. ARCHITECTS.
31 TOOLEY, St. S.E.

REFERENCE:—

A	Wards	H	Administ'n Build'
B	Day E's Wards	K	Water Tower
C	Small Wards	L	Receiving Block
D	Isolation Wards	M	Mortuary
E	Nursing Homes	N	Porters' Lodge
F	Chapel	O	Stable
G	Laundry	P	Corridor

SKETCH PLAN

Negotiations with the Local Government Board continued regarding the provision of sewerage and water supply. The LGB were of the opinion that the rates charges by Croydon were excessive. The LGB had also delayed approval of the plans submitted by Mr Newman despite the Guardians having to pay installments and interest on the loan granted by the Local Government Board. A number of detailed changes were required but eventually permission was given for the contract for the building on 5 September 1901. The contract was signed on 30 October 1901.

The Bermondsey Guardians also built Ladywell Institution for the infirm, opened on 11 July 1901 by the Prince and Princess of Wales, and Bermondsey and Rotherhithe Hospital, later known as St Olave's *(pictured on previous page)*.

"The Shirley Inn" public house, close to the Shirley Schools boundary wall c.1888

CHAPTER TWO

The Bermondsey Board of Guardians

With the land bought, all that remained was to build the Home. Newman & Newman were asked to prepare plans. The buildings comprised 38 cottages, all with names of trees and bushes, from Acacia to Yew. Other buildings were: the school, probationary wards, Headmaster's house, Headmistress' house, staff house, porter's lodge, laundry block, workshops, swimming baths, water tower and infirmary. The Home was self-sufficient in most respects. It included a small farm and even a fire engine.

The contractor, Charles Wall of Ashbwinham Works, Lots Road, Chelsea, was willing to complete the work in eighteen months from the date of commencement. Brown moulded bricks and York stone were the main materials used.

In their Minutes dated October 1903, the Bermondsey Guardians set out the guiding principles of the Home: "A place where the children may receive kindly and homely parental care, a sound education and industrial training to enable them upon leaving the Home to secure a livelihood".

The Schools Committee voted in 1903 to spend £15 annually for newspapers for the children. These included the *Daily Mirror*, *Boys' Own* and *Girls' Own* magazines. It became a tradition that on Derby Day the school's brass band was allowed to play near to the event at Epsom to solicit contributions from racing spectators.

In the spring of 1904 the Headmaster reported to the committee that two young men were charged and prosecuted for stealing lead at the Shirley School building. One of them tried to leave the premises as though he was one of the workmen. Both were convicted at Croydon and sentenced to two months hard labour.

The Southwark Annual for 1905, full of pride for the new institution, remarked how there had been "a model village created, where child life can be trained, free from the physical disadvantages arising from crowded districts, and also from those morally injurious influences which are powerfully demonstrated in the streets of the great metropolis".

The cottages had, on the ground floor, a day room with toys and games for the children, the kitchen where children would eat, lavatories and wash-rooms. Upstairs were two dormitories, one with six and one with eight beds. Another, single bedroom, would be for an older girl who was being trained in domestic service, and another for the Housemother.

There were frequently visits by foreigners, often Germans or Americans, who wanted to look over the establishment. There were also visits by institutions like the Children's Aid Society, the Band of Hope, the South Place Ethical Society and the Amalgamated Society of Engineers. The Guardians either officially encouraged scrutiny or at least did not discourage it. This implies they considered they were running a model institution.

It was an immense task staffing and stocking such a gigantic institution, but everything had to be listed and costed for the Guardians, down to 150 pokers, 45 raisin-stoning machines, and 45 toasting forks.

The Headmaster, John Fergus Henry Roberts, received £150 a year as the highest paid member of staff. He had to be aged between 28 and 45 with previous experience in a Poor Law Institution. The Headmaster would look after the cleanliness of the Home, discipline, diet and Industrial Training. The Headmistress, Miss Capes, would do a similar job for the girls' side of the Home. The lowest paid, 21 year old Clara Girling, employed as a scrubber, had 15s a week, with seven days off a year after she had worked there 12 months.

The other senior post was filled by Mr Coxhead, the clerk and steward, responsible for the stores, farm, engineering, laundry and the fabric of the buildings.

The uniforms for staff and children were also supplied. Boys received one overcoat, two jackets, two vests, two pairs of trousers, two day shirts, three flannel vests, three night shirts, three pairs of socks, one pair of braces, two caps, two neckties, three handkerchiefs and six collars. Girls received two frocks, two upper petticoats, three under petticoats, three combinations, three flannel vests, three night gowns, three pairs of stockings, six pinafores, two hats, six handkerchiefs, one jacket, and one cape. Both received two pairs of boots, one pair of shoes, six small towels and two bath towels.

The amount of food for each person in the institution was carefully rationed. The Headmaster could have 1lb of cheese a week, other officers and servants ½lb. He could have seven pints of milk, they five pints; he one shilling's worth of fruit, they ten pence worth.

Food for the children was allocated according to age. The diet was varied by day so, for example, on a Wednesday a 9–16 year old would receive for breakfast 7oz bread, ³⁄₄oz butter or dripping, 1½oz golden syrup or jam. For dinner (midday) the ration would

be 4oz bread, 4oz cooked meat, 7oz potatoes or other vegetables, 5oz golden pudding or suet pudding or golden syrup or jam roly-poly pudding or rice pudding. For supper: 6oz bread plain or with currants, ³⁄₄oz tea, ³⁄₄oz butter or dripping, 1½oz golden syrup or jam.

It was, therefore, a vitamin-enriched pauper's diet, with the bulk of calories coming from the bread and potatoes. The high level of meat is not remarkable for this time; low quality meat was not expensive and even the poor had long been used to eating meat daily.

The establishment was officially opened on 4 June 1904, under the title The Shirley Schools, Croydon. It had been operating since November 1903, however. The eventual cost was £180,546. The Poor Law Guardians of every location were obsessed with itemised bills and there are impressive tables of comparative costs between the different institutions. Bermondsey was paying 13s (65p) per child a week for its cottage homes in 1908, the highest in a league which included Shoreditch, Greenwich, Poplar, Hackney and Woolwich. Interestingly, 'block schools', like barracks, were not necessarily cheaper, their highest cost being at 14s 5d (72p) for St. Pancras and Strand. Block schools could, however, be run far more cheaply if the Guardians had a mind to do so; the cheapest in the league was one of these, run by Islington, and costing 9s 7d (48p) per child per week.

As time passed, the Schools obtained several horses for farm work, a herd of 20 sheep, a poultry farm and a herd of pigs. A great deal of land was cultivated to provide food for the kitchens: almost all the vegetables were eventually produced on site. Much of the produce, including fresh milk, would come from the farm. Vegetables were grown on the farm by the older boys. Eggs were produced on the premises too, as there were plenty of fowl, but the birds themselves were eaten only by the chief officers.

The site was so large that the Headmaster was allowed to keep a horse and trap, the horse's keep being paid for by the Guardians, so he could make his inspections of daily activities at Shirley.

The Guardians were very proud of their achievement, but the neighbours were less than delighted at the creation of an entire village on what had previously been rolling hills. Mr E. Amsden from the neighbouring property was angry that a "Boys' Workhouse" had been built "as near as possible to a gentleman's house". He replied to complaints of his firing guns near the school grounds that "unless your children stray into my garden, as they have done in the past, no shot or bullet could go near your children".

While ultimate authority rested with the Guardians, they devolved their responsibility to their Children's Homes Committee, sometimes called the Schools Visiting Committee, which consisted of ten people, most of whom were Guardians and who were always referred to as such, so that will be the case in this account.

The Intake

Great strains were placed on the schools by the turnover of children. In the first six months of 1905, for example, 166 children were discharged and 146 were admitted. All the new children had to be assessed and fitted into a class. Elizabeth Smith, aged 12 and admitted in August 1905, "scarcely knows the alphabet and states that she has not attended school for years". Sidney, George and Samuel H. were admitted in October 1905. Aged 9, 10 and 11, they were said to have "no educational knowledge whatsoever". Children were admitted who did not know their own birth date. For administrative ease they were reckoned as from July 1 in the year most likely to be the year of their birth.

The usual number of children in the Schools was around 550. In February 1907, for example, there were 548: 272 in the boys' cottages; 238 in the girls'; 10 in the infirmary and 28 in the probationary wards.

The children were received from the workhouse via a children's home in Peckham, which seems to have been a holding centre. The state of some of them is demonstrated by a report by Dr J. B. Ridley, who had to send back some children in March 1907, "as they were suffering from bad eyes, itch and impetigo...Many of the children have very dirty legs and feet, and one child had foul smelling feet; another child had a highly

Original school building at Shirley

School assembly 1907

Boys and girls in the school playground 1907

offensive condition of the mouth due to extensive ulceration. There have also been several cases of broken chilblains, which I regret to say were sent down without any dressings on them, the result being that the stockings are stuck to the sores, which must cause great pain, considering that these children walked from Woodside Station to Shirley Schools."

The Medical Officer from the Peckham Homes responded: "You must remember that we receive children to the homes in all sorts of conditions from Parish Street workhouse, and we have no power of selection, but have simply to admit what is sent to us. Many of these children have been sadly neglected and half-starved, so that their condition is poor." He noted that of 160 children transferred in four months, only six had been rejected on medical grounds.

The Headmaster admitted 25 boys aged 5-13 in July 1904 and noted: "After 23 years experience with all classes of boys, I can safely assert that in educational slackness, vicious mischievous conduct and immoral language and behaviour, this batch of boys is by far the worst I have had to deal with."

Children were adopted by the Guardians when parents resisted voluntary care but might be a danger to the children. Thus the

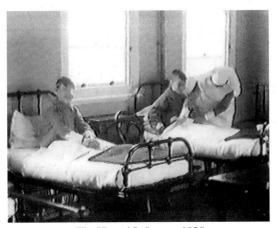
The Homes' Infirmary 1929

five children aged 3-14 of Rose S., 34, were adopted when she was given a year's hard labour for "concealment of birth". This sentence always meant infanticide: to prove murder it was necessary to prove the child had been born alive, and this was rarely possible, so "concealment" carried a stiff penalty.

Housemothers

The general regulations for housemothers sprang from the basic philosophy of Shirley Schools: "kindly and homely parental care, a sound education, and industrial training".

Housemothers had 14 or 15 children each, but children were expected to do a good deal of the household work, so the job was less onerous than might be thought. They were to attend to all the children's needs and had the right to requisition any items they needed.

Housemothers were sometimes prepared to take the children's side against teachers. The Headmaster recorded on 2 April 1904 that he had received "an impertinent letter" from a housemother, Miss Smith, concerning a reprimand a girl in her cottage had received for general untidiness. The following month he remarked on "an insolent letter" from a housemother over a similar incident. He clearly considered the teaching staff to be superior to the Housemothers, though he did write to teachers to tell them not to communicate with house parents, adding, "it is my desire that you deal as tactfully as possible with all cases of personal untidiness and uncleanliness".

The general instructions for housemothers informed them: "It is by a kindly and sympathetic control and treatment, and by good example and checking small faults rather than by any system of severity, that the occurrence, as far as possible, of any serious misbehaviour is to be avoided. Fathers and Mothers [the instructions were written when there were housefathers] must fully realise that the success in after-life of the children will depend in a great measure upon their influence and example."

In the Home's early years housemothers had a dark striped dress covered by an apron for use in the mornings and a black surge dress for the afternoons. Later the afternoon uniform was changed to a navy blue frock.

The schools started with the double cottages being presided over by a house-mother and housefather, who were married, aided by assistant housemothers. This did not work; housemothers made their assistants to do all the work, and the housefathers had no suitable role, so the practice was discontinued.

The Day

There were strict instructions that two children must never be allowed to sleep in the same bed. Other rules were that children must wash at least three times a day and be bathed at least once a day. Baths had to be not less than 88 degrees fahrenheit and not more than 98 degrees. Children's hair must be combed once a day.

The day began at 6am with a screeching steam siren, like those used to signal factory workers. The neighbours complained to Beck-enham Urban District Council, but the sole concession of the Headmaster was to halve the duration of the whistle.

The children would be washed and dressed and would have breakfast and prayers at 7.30am. Older children in industrial training and work would start at 8am, the school would start at 8.50am. School and industrial work would stop at midday for a meal at 12.25pm. Afternoon work would start at 1pm and school would start at 1.50pm. School would end at 3.40pm, work at 5pm and industrial training at 5.30pm. There would be supper at 5.30pm when house mothers were encouraged to "converse with the children on passing events or subjects of common interest". There would be evening schools for those in industrial training. Except for these children, from 6pm until bed-time would be free time. Bed-time was 7pm for children under eight, and 8pm for the older ones. Lights in the rooms were out no later than 9pm, and all the cottage lights were expected to be out by 10.30pm.

Typical double cottage at Shirley

School

There were ten classes (known as standards) plus infants. Progress up the standards was by academic ability, so there would be children of roughly the same ability but different ages. If a child was not felt able to keep up, he would be sent down. Thus James B. was transferred from standard II to standard I, "he being mentally weak and a fit subject for a special difficulty school".

The Schools' Inspector's report in 1904 was headed "Shirley Cottage Homes School (Bermondsey Union)". He noted: "The children passed an excellent examination... the whole establishment is at present conducted with marked energy."

The Schools received a certificate of 'Excellent' in all subjects. This was the highest award ever given to a poor law school.

A child of about 11 years old would be taking lessons in reading, geography, mental arithmetic, recitation, history and music.

Nature study was a favourite subject, involving plant recognition, natural

Shirley Schools c.1929. The Board of Guardians thought that 300 children was the maximum number for a school but Bermondsey wanted places for 600, therefore the plan had to suggest two schools, each of 300.

geography, the weather, development of insects, and plant fertilisation though not animal reproduction. Reading books included *The Mill on the Floss, Ivanhoe, The Last Days of Pompeii* and *Uncle Tom's Cabin.* Art included pastel work, lead pencil, memory drawing and clay modelling. Elementary science was taught involving heat and its effects, the three states of matter and so on, all under the general heading of 'engineering'. The history syllabus started with Celtic Britain, Aryan Race and Homes, then Romans in Britain. There was a great deal of emphasis on the wars with France, up to the Napoleonic war, and on the growth of the British Empire.

Girls would be expected to pass examinations in basic needlework – cutting out a simple garment in paper and material or knitting socks on four needles. The Inspector suggested girls as well as boys should be taught swimming in 1904 and this was put into effect.

Inspectors reports were published in the local newspapers. In March 1908 the inspector criticised the art class, "especially in drawing with the brush(a tendency to rely too much upon flat examples". The report was generally positive, and also advised "that the younger girls should have some share in the drawing lessons; that some simple oral lessons in history should be given; that older children should, to a greater extent, be encouraged to acquire information for themselves from their books, and that a rather more practical turn should be given to the arithmetic".

Tailoring workshop, 1907

Pupils in industrial training would continue academic education in evening classes three days a week from 5.45pm to 7.45pm These classes included shorthand, historical reading, geographical reading, letter writing, and hygiene for girls, while boys did mechanics.

In 1910 a circular was sent round instructing how girls must be taught hygiene. Between 7 and 12 they must be taught the value of "fresh air and ventilation; dealing with the necessity for fresh air; the effective ventilation of a room; the need for open windows by night as well as by day; some effects of living in ill-ventilated rooms; the value of sunshine". They were also given lessons on 'temperance', 'washing and dressing a baby' and the 'feeding of infants', but nothing on menstruation, childbirth or contraception.

In this era before the First World War, when male workers were plentiful, light office jobs were done by men, not women as later became the case, so it is unsurprising to see the boys excelling in shorthand – Frank Ogier and Robert Gepheart took the Pitman's Shorthand examination in 1912. In 1916 the prizes for shorthand and typing were both won by Charles Purnell.

Children had exercise books for their finished work but for classwork and general working out they still used slates until 1913.

Health

There were frequent sore throats, which were believed to be caused by the dampness of the site, resulting from the lack of surface drainage, so drainage channels were dug.

Epidemics of childhood diseases were viewed with a natural terror. When there was measles in Shirley in 1911, the village was declared out of bounds. Children were kept away from school with chicken pox, diphtheria, mumps and whooping cough.

Scarlet fever was treated with drastic action. In 1912 the schools were closed between 9

Swimming, for both boys and girls, was introduced in 1904. In this 1929 picture pupils are receiving instructions in diving styles.

February and 12 April because of an epidemic of scarlet fever, but they had been too hasty in re-opening and a more serious outbreak then occurred, necessitating a further closure between 24 May and 8 July. An average of 80 children were absent from July until the end of October, staying at the South Eastern Children's Hospital.

All the infected children's bedding and clothing had to be burned. The walls were whitewashed and painted. Elsewhere the buildings were cleansed, the school whitewashed and the stock disinfected to get rid of the scarlet fever bacteria. It was through such thorough measures all over the country that scarlet fever in its virulent form was wiped out, for the bacteria had nowhere to live.

Children were cautioned: "especially the girls, against wearing each other's hats and using each other's brushes and combs, as this practice promotes the spread of ringworm."

If ringworm was a serious condition, the cure could be even worse. The treatment included X-rays, but staff did not always take adequate care. In April 1910, the Medical Officer, Dr Ridley, reported on two children, Alice C. and Ellen C., who would be permanently bald as a result of the treatment. In March 1924 he wrote a new report: "From time to time since that date, children have been returned after X-ray treatment with burnt heads. At the present date there are seven children in the schools who are permanently disfigured for the rest of their lives. Two of them can never be sent out into the world without wearing a wig. I can only regard this matter as a scandal…It shows either great carelessness or professional incom-petence in the handling of the X-ray apparatus…If such a condition as this happened to any child in private life, an action would be brought by the parents and the result would be heavy damages." The seven children injured ranged from 6 year old Charles D., 'quite bald', to 13 year old Florence H.,'partly bald.' They had all been treated at the Goldie Leigh Hospital (with one exception). The Guardians agreed to supply wigs and not to send any further children to Goldie Leigh for treatment.

Some children arrived with terminal conditions. Lilian Simmons, 12, was admitted in March 1911 suffering from "Tuberculosis peritonitis of long standing". She was transferred to Rotherhithe Infirmary, where she died ten days later. Two six year old boys were brought in at the same time suffering from spinal curvature as a result of tuber-culosis of the spine.

Sometimes children died from conditions which seemed to be minor. James Nash, aged 10, died on 15 February 1909 from a broken chilblain which became infected and led to septicaemia (blood poisoning). His mother, a domestic servant in Dover, was telegraphed to inform her how ill he was, but she arrived after his death.

On 10 December 1918, the Medical Officer stated: "I have to report the death of Dorothy Ward, aged 13 years, on 25 November from influenza and pneumonia. This makes the seventh death since the opening of the schools in 1903." If children were known to be seriously ill they would be transferred to Rotherhithe & Bermondsey District Hospital or Mayday in Croydon, because they would receive better care and because of the effect on the morale of the staff and children of someone dying at the Home.

Religion
Religion was an important part of life at Shirley Schools. There were prayers at breakfast, then a hymn sung when children had reached their classes in school along with the Lord's Prayer and a benediction. At midday, each class sang grace. At the end of school there was another hymn, followed by the Lord's Prayer and a benediction. There would be grace with the evening meal and prayers before bedtime.

The youngest children had to know the Lord's Prayer, three hymns and the catechism to the end of the Creed. Older children learned the Ten Commandments, the 23rd Psalm and Matthew V. 1-12 by heart, and were instructed in the Old and New Testaments.

A frequent comment of the Schools' Inspector was that examinations of 'repetition' were "well known, but lacking in intelligent appreciation of the subject matter".

The report on religious instruction made clear "suitable opportunity should be supplied for inculcating industry, sobriety and thrift, and such principles of virtue should be urged by example, warnings, cautions and admonitions".

Nina Forster in *Growth of a Parish* stated:

"The Vicar of St. John's, Shirley, was appointed Chaplain to the schools. He conducted a Service for the children each Sunday afternoon in the school building. Later on, the older children were marched to church for Matins every Sunday, led by the School band, filling the seats in the North Aisle. The Headmaster, Mr Roberts, drove to church with his wife and daughter in a 'dog cart'.

In 1913 the children still marched to church on Sunday mornings and from Baptism and Confirmation records, the Schools chaplain certainly took his ministry at the Schools seriously. Between 1912 and 1918 the average annual number of Baptisms rose from 15 to over 60 accounted for by mass services prior to Confirmation. The maximum baptised at one service was 93 in 1916! The chaplain of the Home, the Rev. George Jones would not consider candidates for Confirmation without evidence of Baptism, not easy to produce in the case of children at Shirley Schools."

At that time it was taken for granted that all children at Shirley should become members of the Church of England. There was neither Nonconformist nor Roman Catholic chaplain.

Morality

There was "an experimental lesson on alcohol to the upper standards" in September 1904. This does not seem to have been repeated, perhaps because of the danger of exciting interest in the product being warned against.

In another lecture, "the use of bad language was strongly condemned, and the scholars were advised, in every instance, to report the culprit, without delay, to any officer of the school staff".

The Headmaster paid particular attention to the boys, giving them a "general exhortation, especially those soon leaving, affecting their character and well-being as men... [He] gave them practical advice as to attending evening schools, places of worship, avoiding bad companions."

He was forever giving moral lectures to the boys, emphasising things like "the necessity of

Shirley Prize Band on church parade 1907

energy, pushfulness and the exercise of character whilst in the cricket or football fields, the workshops, and especially when leaving the schools to gain their own livelihood".

In June 1911 he lectured them on "the lessons to be learned from the lives of men well known to them, who have risen from poverty to positions of affluence through industry and perseverance."

Pride in the British Empire and devotion to King and Country were important aspects of moral education. On Empire Day the Headmaster told the teachers to "allow the children to sing some suitably patriotic songs".

The older pupils presumably had the same needs as other adolescents, though the coy language makes it difficult to establish exactly what was happening. "The boy, Charles P., was reported by Mr Wright for a filthy action, and I punished him" was perhaps a punishment for masturbation, though it could just as easily have been, say, urinating in a public place. Stanley W., aged 13, who had been sent back to the workhouse "for depraved habits", was returned when "the master of the workhouse reports the boy has recovered therefrom".

In a very unusual case, Elizabeth M. was called to see her son, George, almost 14, because "serious allegations had been made as to the moral character of her son. That he was in consequence unfit to remain in the school". She saw him and wrote to the Guardians that he was "very dejected and upset". She could gain "no authentic information from him as to the charges made against him, but gathered from him that he was treated quite differently from any other boy. That he had been unaware of doing anything wrong, but he had been successful in gaining prizes and that other boys were jealous of him. His prizes had been taken from him and he was very unhappy. It seems a reasonable guess from this jumbled story that George was homosexual. He was discharged to the workhouse, then to his mother.

The contamination of other children by the "depravity" of some was feared. Rose A., aged 12, was sent to the Metropolitan Asylums Board with a form marked "defective", because she was "very troublesome, steals everything she sees, was morally depraved and not fit to be with other children". The Board rejected her as she was not "feeble-minded" and she was sent to the workhouse.

There are no reports of sexual assaults by any of the staff on children, which may mean none took place, because the moral code held up, or that the moral code prevented children from talking about abuses which had taken place. Sexual misbehaviour among the children was dealt with severely. Charles Q., 14, was charged in 1927 with "interfering with girls. The Matron reported him for indecent behaviour and threatening to use a knife on Gladys M. of Daisy Cottage, aged 14, at the rear of the workshops". The Housemother gave evidence to the Children's Homes Committee, stating that Gladys M. alleged that the boy had threatened her with a knife, wanting her to undress. The Housemother continued, however, that she "understood the girl M. was not a very good girl, and in her opinion it was not all the boy's fault, and that she would not be surprised if it was not a pre-arranged meeting". Asked to put his side of things, Q. virtually admitted trying to lift up M's clothes and threatening her with a penknife. He was transferred to the National Nautical School at Portishead, where discipline was strict and, presumably, there were no girls.

Discipline
On 16 March 1904 the Headmaster wrote: "Thomas Phillips was reported for punishment, his offence being careless work. This is the first case of punishment since the opening of the school 18 months ago".

The Headmaster complained that respect shown by "the raising of a boy's cap" or "the stepping on one side to make way" were notably absent. If these were the infringements he felt he must warn about, the school was very well behaved although in one day, 21 girls were reported to the Headmaster for being 15 minutes late at school, so it cannot be said that everyone adhered to a military discipline.

In May 1906 there was a report that Jane Childs (13 or 14) "has been constantly reported by her various teachers for general bad conduct, especially sullenness. She has been frequently spoken to by myself and the staff. Today she was caught in the act of reading the private notes in the school's diary."

In a report on corporal punishment in June 1907, the Headmaster noted it was inflicted on boys only, "with either a cane or a birch rod. During the five years in which I have had control of the schools, the latter has been used only once." Punishment was inflicted by the Headmaster or the First Assistant Master. Only once was a female child beaten and then the housemother involved "was summarily dismissed". In 1909 the Headmaster forbade the punishment of children by standing them in the corridor outside classes. In 1912 he castigated "the deplorable manner of speaking prevalent among the children. This more especially refers to the girls, for their mumbling and mincing way of talking has become intolerable."

A report of suspected cruelty found its way into the *South London Press* on 28 January 1905 after two women attendants were dismissed, "in consequence of a child in their care found with bruises about the neck and body – a very delicate boy of about four years old. One of the women had admitted slapping the boy and both bathed him during their duty.

Relatives
The housemothers were forbidden to have any communication with relatives of the children and no visits were permitted except on Visiting Day. To begin with this was the third Thursday in the month, but visits were later much curtailed. All letters to or from the children had to be sent through the Headmaster or Mistress, and envelopes had to bear the initial of the housemother to show she had examined it.

There was a warning to teachers that "children, particularly boys, when being marched to church, are allowed to break the line and to have interviews with relatives who occasionally hang about the school gates on Sundays. The Guardians very much object to this promiscuous visiting."

Some attempts were made to remove children from the pernicious influence of parents, but some proposals went too far. The Guardians of Newcastle wrote in 1911 that they were "desirous of exchanging children at present in their Home whose parents or relatives are likely to exercise an evil influence over their after-life, for an equal number of similar children from Unions in different parts of the country" and asking whether the Guardians were prepared to consider such an exchange. The reply was terse:"in our opinion the difficulties are very great and the advantages small. We do not consider it desirable to make such arrangements."

Visiting was always a problem, as the prevailing view was that since the parents were not supporting their children, they had little right of access, if any. This caused obvious distress. A widow, Mrs Rask, with two of her six children at Shirley, wrote in November 1910 to the Guardians that she had first been told she could see them every three months. "Since then they have restricted the visiting to two hours every six months, because some of the mothers (they said) were intoxicated on visiting day. It is hard enough for a mother who loves her children to have to part with them, but to be debarred from seeing them for six months, I think it is scandalous."

In considering this, it was repeated that there had been incidents of "disorderly conduct, unseemly behaviour and drunkenness", but the Guardians agreed to bar only those guilty of these offences and revert to three monthly visits for all others.

The Home was segregated by sex, but brothers and sisters were permitted to visit each other's cottages at certain hours on Sundays. The Guardians liked to maintain contact with parents from whom they could expect a contribution to their funds. On 5 May 1925 there was an application by Henry L. to have his child Eugene, 5, who was at the Hollies transferred to Shirley. He was already paying 2s 6d weekly for William, a child already at Shirley.

Parents had some influence if the Guardians had not adopted children. Thus Fred Tarrant, 13, who played in the band, was up for enlistment into the army as a band boy. His mother, Eliza, a 52 year old widow, wrote to him on 2 October 1906: "Should the authorities or the school or teacher ask or try to persuade you to be a soldier, you must refuse. I have been asked several times about it and have refused each time…It would be so much nicer for you to be at home. If you were, I should be so much happier and so also would you. With love from all." He was discharged later to her care.

Efforts were made to keep the children from their relatives, even after they had left the schools. As the Headmaster wrote in a report about employment in December 1911: "As the boys in this parish are Londoners and to disassociate them as much as possible from the district of their birth and associations, which may interfere with the prospects afforded them by the Guardians, I invariably place them in the provinces."

To some extent, the Home operated as a cheap childminding service for the desperately poor or simply for single parents whose work took them away from home.

Training

'Technical schools' were started in 1905 to ease the transition between school and work. They included carpentry; plumbing and gas fitting; engineering and smith's work; tailoring; shoemaking; gardening (including vegetable growing); and poultry keeping. In 1910 the metal workshop was expanded to include tin plate, lead and other metals.

After the school had been running for some years, 'store keeping' and 'office routine' were added to the subjects for which there was training.

At the age of 14, children were transferred to the work division where training was continuous and efforts were made to find them suitable 'situations'. The best placement was when a boy could be sent to work as an apprentice and given bed and board plus a sum of money while he learned a trade which could keep him for the rest of his life.

For 'cookery and housewifery', older girls divided into groups of six and spent a whole day each week at the house where the staff lived, receiving "practical teaching and actual practice", that is, they did the clerical staff's housework.

Provision was made for every girl to have 15 months' training in domestic work prior to going into service. A girl in advanced training would live in her own bedroom, for which she was responsible, and would learn such domestic arts as washing woollens and starching linen. Domestic skills were highly valued and girls were awardd prizes — at prize day in 1919, for example, Annie Wafer was awarded the prize as "best domestic servant".

On the other hand, "some of the dullest girls go into laundries. If a girl is not thought intelligent enough to make a domestic servant, she is sent for ten months into the laundry, in order to become mechanically efficient in that work."

There was a boys' band of 36, who found it easy to enter the services equipped with the skill of playing a musical instrument. 'Band boys' had to practise frequently, to the irritation of Mr Amsden, the neighbour who complained: "Last Sunday the so-called Band played for a long time and never in tune or together." It cannot have been all that bad, as

Boys acquiring skills in carpentry and, below, the girls practise ironing and pressing, 1907

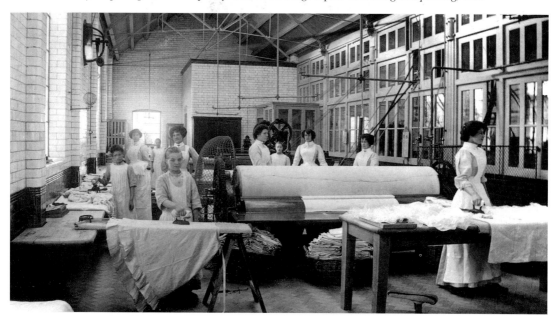

in May 1905 the band was asked by Croydon Council to play in the public park on Saturdays for one guinea per performance. They always led the Church parade on Sundays. Favourite tunes were The March and The Director. These were to become signature tunes for the Home.

The *Southwark Annual* for 1905 proclaimed:

"It is surprising, when one considers their ages (from 11 to 14), what splendid music can be produced from such raw material with careful training. Their repertoire is indeed an extensive one, and they obtain many engagements in the surrounding district, and the boys are greatly sought after by military bands. One boy went to India last summer to serve in the band of the 2nd Warwickshire, and the regiment is to be congratulated upon having secured the services of the youth, Goodfellow by name, who is a cornet player of exceeding promise."

Work

On going to situations, a girl would set off, supplied with a regulation serge dress, with an upper petticoat, under petticoat, combinations and a series of aprons for different kinds of work: six coarse, two muslin, two hessian. Their wages were set at £8 a year, and

Cobblers' workshop, 1907

the clothes were not their own until they had been in service a year.

Many servants would be supplied direct to a single employer who wanted a 'general help', a 'between maid' or a 'kitchen maid'. Mrs H Ringer from Chislehurst, for example, wrote to the Schools on 9 February 1907: "If you have a nice, quiet girl, I shall be pleased to take her. Clean and neat in appearance and habits and perfectly good temper, and I should like her as soon as you can get her ready. I need hardly tell you she will have a good home, and her health and comfort studied. Please impress upon her before she comes that my rules and orders must be strictly obeyed, and that she will not be allowed out at nights, not even to Church, all the Winter evenings. I do not consider it right for young girls to be out in the dark."

The Metropolitan Association for Befriending Young Servants (MABYS) would visit the girls at least once in the first year. They would try to sort out problems like that of Daisy Dark, 17, in a house in Havelock Road, East Croydon, who complained: "The work of the house is getting too much for her, that her wages are the same as when she first started in June 1905, and that she has only had one half day holiday in four months."

MABYS thus seems to have been acting as a moral police force, keeping a control over girls until well into maturity. Presumably such control could be exercised until the girls reached 21, which was legal adulthood.

Since wage differentials were based on age, employers would choose the younger worker rather than an older worker who had two extra years of schooling, but was similarly inexperienced. Also, some occupations like the post office and army bands, closed recruitment at 16.

Some girls do not seem to have been born for a life of domestic service. Mrs Alice Barnes of West Hampstead, wrote of Mary Davey, 15, that "within the last month she has broken 11 cups (breakfast and tea cups), 13 glasses of three sizes, water bottles, plates innumerable, meat dishes, burnt three socks which were airing and finally, yesterday, I discovered when she went to the store cupboard to fetch a simple piece of soap, she managed to smash a beautiful large dish which will cost me 7s 6d to replace."

Mary Manlove of the Royal Female Philanthropic Society, which was overseeing this placement in the manner of MABYS, added in her own report that: "She does nothing at all when left by herself except make herself look very black…She will not get up in the morning". A later age would consider this normal adolescent behaviour. Mary Davey was sent for a year to the Dudley Stuart Training Home, presumably a place of more rigorous training than Shirley Schools provided.

Much more care was taken with the training and placement of boys, as it was thought that the girls would soon marry, have babies and give up work, while boys would have to earn money for their families. The Headmaster in December 1911 reported that 25% of boys entered the army as bandsmen; 5% became boy seamen; 7½% of "intelligent and refined but somewhat delicate boys" went into office work; 15% showed no aptitude for any trade: "They may be dull, indolent or contrary, and are then placed with miners in South Wales." The rest were sent to the trades in which they had been trained as apprentices.

The Guardians' Enquiry Officer was far from impressed with the standard of living of the boys who were sent to Wales. "Nearly every lad…is living practically from hand to mouth" and he refers to "the utterly unscrupulous

A girls Cottage group, 1907

nature of some of the applicants for boys". Frequently the miners they lived with took almost all their earnings for board and lodgings and other expenses.

Each boy was given an outfit with a tin trunk, on the inner lid of which was a message saying if the boy should be in need of a friend, he could apply to "The Secretary, Association for Befriending Boys, Denison House, 296 Vauxhall Bridge Road, S.W."

It was sometimes difficult for the Headmaster to judge what was happening when a placement looked as if it would break down, and he was as well to bide his time. A nursery owner called Samuel Iremonger from Slough, wrote about a boy called Frank Still, in June 1904, that he: "absolutely refused to work from the day he came. Asked his reason, he replied that he wished to be a shoemaker, not a gardener, and that he was not asked what he wished to be. Has bolted twice…I should suggest a training ship for such a very stubborn lad." Still did run away and was found by an officer of the Church Army, who wrote to the Headmaster that he had found him an apprenticeship with a baker, where he was quite happy, and that at Iremonger's "I feel sure he was used rather rough." Confirmation of this view came from the police about another boy, Philip Wingrove, 15, found "wandering apparently destitute at Slough" as Samuel Iremonger had thrown him out. He was sent no more boys.

Employers grumbled frequently about their boys. To quote from a range of different letters in 1907: "sullen in manner", "his only desire seems to be getting away with other boys"; "he should have gone to stay with his

A boys Cottage group, outside Myrtle and Musk Cottage, 1907

sister, but he did not go there but loafed about this street", "stayed with people reported to be of very questionable character in the neighbourhood", "most unwilling and ignorant." Despite this disapproval, the ultimate rejection rate was low. Three boys were reported as being rejected by their employers: one was dishonest, one because he was "not quick enough" for work on a book stall, and another for "repulsive appearance".

The Guardians or the Headmaster also received grateful letters, like one from Priscilla F. Green, after she had been in service seven months in Somerton. She wrote: "I do not know how to thank the Guardians of the Shirley Schools enough. I was in the schools nearly four years, and I think that they have always done their best for me. My brothers and sister in the Shirley Schools often write to me and tell me how happy they are. I am so far away that I feel it more because I cannot see the ones whom I love."

Henry Tickell, apprenticed to a butcher, wrote in October 1913: "I received my rise three weeks ago, and am now getting five shillings a week…I am very grateful to you for getting me such a good situation."

This was good money. Farm boys' wages went from 2s a week to 3s 6d. Still, some boys liked the life. Arthur Kirk wrote to the Headmaster from Glamorgan in 1920: "If you want to see a strong farmer, come and see George Studdard. He is big, strong, healthy and robust, and I cannot say too much for such a young giant as he. Dick Smith grows like a weed, very tall and thin, and Fred Sparks is a little dwarf that won't grow. As for myself, I am growing slowly but strong, so that gives you an idea of what a jolly lot of farmers we will make."

Many more letters of complaint than pleasure are on record, but this is probably because there was a natural tendency for former pupils to be moved to write if they had a problem rather than if they were content. It is also difficult to quote from many letters of thanks in that they are rather dull and cloying. This follows from the truism that happy people are more or less alike in their happiness, but each misery has its own character.

A report for the three years ending in December 1916 broke down the figures for 87 girls who had been sent out to service. Of the 69 who had left their first situation, 26 had gone to relatives and friends, 15 it was not possible to trace, 4 were in rescue homes, 3 in MABYS homes, 21 were in other situations.

Of the boys, 67 had gone into service and 45 had left. 16 went with friends and relatives, 15 joined the services, 7 it was impossible to trace and 7 obtained other situations. It should be noted, however, that these were war years, when labour was in short supply and even those relatively unskilled young people could pick and choose their employers in a way which was not possible in peacetime.

Sometimes the records read as if the Home was a factory for producing disciplined workers. Probably neither the Guardians nor the senior staff would have considered this in any way improper. They wanted to produce young people who could look after themselves, lead moral lives, and not end up in the workhouse like many of their parents.

The schools had a 'recreation fund', which was drawn on in April 1907 for "1 gross tops and cord for same, 2,000 marbles and one box alleys for the sum of 11s 3d, 3 doz. battledores and shuttle cocks; skipping ropes, wooden hoops and balls for the sum of £1 0s 6d."

Children participated in the annual flower show in the village where, it was announced: "The girls will exhibit various garments made in the schools, while the boys can show drawings and skill in the collection and arrangement of wild flowers and grasses."

Sports Day 1908 included, for visitors, an inspection of the school, trade shops and handicrafts, laundry, farm, garden, poultry farm, allotments and cottages. The brass band played and there was a dumb-bell drill by a squad of boys, a gymnastic display, exhibition of school work, art, needlework and a wild flower competition. The school choir sang and other performances included elocution, swimming and a life-saving competition. There were prizes for wild flower displays, cottage gardens, all handicrafts, including plumbing and engineering, laundry work and mending and darning. The day was rounded off with God Save the King.

At Christmas 1908 there was an evening entertainment which consisted of dances and songs like 'Little Girlies from Japan' and 'Could We But Rule', and the second part was a play, The Sleeping Beauty. Following this, the Christmas entertainment, with professionally printed programmes, became a regular

fixture. There were also visits to the pantomime at the Theatre Royal, Croydon.

People from the workhouses and Poor Law Schools were specifically invited by the King to view the coronation procession on 29 June 1911. There was a ballot for the 45 places allotted to Shirley Schools. Later, 220 children went to Crystal Palace to see the Festival of Empire and the Pageant of London. The caterer J. Lyons donated a glass of milk and a large bun to each child.

There would frequently be visiting lecturers, as in October 1911, when Professor Hunter gave a talk on 'Ants and their Work'.

At Christmas 1911 the schools closed early to allow 256 children to attend the Picture Palace in Croydon. The editor of the magazine *Truth* always sent presents: 3d to schoolchildren and 6d to workers. Old boys

Girl's hockey team, 1907

were welcomed back for a reunion on Boxing Day, and took part in a soccer match for 'past and present' scholars.

In 1911 the school's teams were withdrawn from the Poor Law Sports League. The Headmaster complained of unsportsmanlike behaviour by teams from other schools, which was condoned by their staff. Other things troubled him too. At the swimming display, "one school arrived equipped with a gallon of oil with which to anoint the bodies of the children. They also had their muscles massaged after each race, while they were treated after the style of professional athletes." He felt the most successful schools spent "far too much time in training a few specially able children, while the rest of the scholars suffer."

He replaced this with a 'cottage league' for Shirley. There were 609 children at Shirley Schools at that time. On annual sports days, or when cottages were engaged in any activity against each other, the school was divided into four groups, named after famous authors and denoted by coloured sashes worn by the competitors. The house names were Barry (red), Dickens (yellow), Kingsley (blue) and Stevenson (green).

Emigration

Few, if any, boys were 'emigrated' to Canada in the first years of the School until, in 1907, a relationship developed with the Catholic Emigration Association which would organise emigration for £12 a head on production of a health certificate and a declaration before a Justice of the Peace that they were willing to emigrate. The details were all filled out on forms headed 'Emigration of Orphan and

Boy's cricket team, 1907

Deserted Pauper Children to Canada'. Sometimes parents refused to give their permission, as in the case of the father of John Hensby, 14, but as the man was in Tanner Street workhouse and had three children chargeable to the Guardians, it was agreed that the consent of the father would not be required.

Certainly some settled happily in Canada. Joseph Lane wrote to his younger brother, Edward, 14: "Just a few lines to let you know I am in the best of health and doing plenty of work at present. I am sending you four shillings and two pence at this time. I am going to fetch you out here to live with me… Do not smoke cigarettes or anything else." The younger boy later filled in emigration forms and wrote thanking the Guardians for their help when he left.

Subsidence

On 19 March 1915 a lengthy report was submitted to the Guardians with reference to a number of subsidence at the Home. It appeared that settlements were due to clay soil on which the Home was built, with heavy rains after some years of comparatively dry weather. In 1908 the Guardians spent £140 9s 8d on pinning the buildings. They spent a further £385 4s 8d on similar work on seven buildings. The Guardians happily agreed to pay the bills of the builder, architect and geological expert.

The First World War

The first effect of the war was that holidays were curtailed and some members of staff who were in the Territorial Army were called up. The Headmaster addressed the senior children and told them to do their duty, by "taking care of their clothing, and in not wasting food and other necessaries". On Empire Day 1915 he reported: "I spoke of the many Shirley boys doing their share in their country's needs, and spoke a word of sympathy in regard to our wounded."

Children were told at assemblies of old boys killed in action, wounded or taken prisoner.

Teachers all made a contribution from their wages to the Prince of Wales Fund for those experiencing hardship due to the war. Soon a shortage of teachers and an increase in pupils because of the war meant classrooms were overcrowded.

Some soldiers would write to the Headmaster from the front, like H. J. Confort who wrote of his school days in October 1915: "To tell you the truth, sir, I often wish I was back experiencing those good times over again, because one very often finds it a hard task to go the straight road through life in the army at the present time."

The Schools Committee report in early 1915 read: "Having sent for the past 12 years a number of our brightest boys into Army bands annually, it is needless to point out to you the fact that a very large number of these Bermondsey lads are now giving valuable assistance in their country's need. Of course, many of those who have enlisted during the last two or three years are too young for active service, but a very large number are fighting in Flanders, or on the seas. Hardly a day passes too, but what I hear news of some young man, a former Shirley scholar (who has been placed out by the Guardians into civilian life), having joined the forces as a volunteer. It would take too long for me to record particulars of all the visits I have received from soldiers who formerly resided here, most of them coming to say goodbye to the schools, the staff and myself, before plunging into the unknown. I have sad news of others of our boys since your last meeting, and one glorious item of news – an item of which I am sure you will all be proud.

Reuben Baldwin – who was enlisted 17 November 1905 in the band of 2nd Worcester Regiment (which was then stationed at Ceylon Barrack, Colombo), and who subsequently rose to the rank of Corporal, has won the

Distinguished Conduct Medal for bravery on the field of battle. As you are aware, this ranks next to the Victoria Cross, and is usually for conduct which merits the latter award.

I regret to have to report the deaths of the following former scholars:

Charles Edwards — Enlisted from the schools into the Band of the First Rifle Brigade, 26 November 1906, and who was killed in the trenches of Flanders. He had risen to the rank of Corporal, was a pupil from Kneller Hall, and while a most capable young man, his bravery earned him the reputation of being the dare-devil of his regiment.

Edward Clarke – Enlisted from the schools, 31 October 1911, as a boy Seaman, and joined HMS "Impregnable". He was subsequently invalided out, and had since joined the Rifle Brigade. He was killed in the trenches in Flanders by a "dum-dum" bullet, and fell by the side of another Shirley boy – Harry Dark – who, by the way, assisted to bury him, and was shot through the leg, and returned home wounded. He is now convalescent, and came to see me a few days' ago.

John Simpson – Enlisted from the schools, 25 October 1909, into His Majesty's Navy, and was lost when HMS "Amphion" went down off the Suffolk coast.

Alfred Glass – Enlisted 30 October 1907 into the Band of the First Rifle Brigade, and was killed in the same trench as Charles Edwards.

Benjamin Walker – Enlisted 17 December 1905, into the 2nd Worcester Regiment, and was shot dead by a sniper, near Armentières.

Three other old boys had been killed in action. George Pritchard, II Batt, Kings Own Royal Lancashire; George Cornish of the same regiment and Henry Doyle, 1st Batt.

I regret exceedingly having to report the loss of these splendid young fellows, but I am keeping a careful record of the Shirley Boys, and their part in the Great War in which our country is engaged, with a view to suitably memorising their names, at some future time."

Shirley saw its own action on 13 October 1915 when there was a zeppelin raid on Croydon. At 11.30pm "deafening reports were heard – 9 or 10 in succession, accompanied by huge flashes of light. The concussion was enormous, and the buildings appeared to shake, while the windows rattled...The children behaved, there was no panic or even crying." The children went down to the sitting rooms of their cottages and waited with their housemothers until 1.30am, when they went back to bed.

The War Office occupied the water tower at Shirley, and monopolised the Headmaster's telephone, which irritated him no end. On 1 May 1917, a Lieutenant Humphreys had to bring his aeroplane down near the schools. It was repaired and he left the next day.

In March 1917 the Guardians awarded prizes for 'good conduct' to children engaged in growing potatoes, cabbages, rhubarb, turnips and other vegetables. They were allowed 4d a week in War Saving Certificates. However, by 1924 the District Auditor and the Ministry of Health disapproved of the scheme, so it was abolished.

On 24 May 1917 the Headmaster appealed for children not to run on the grass, which was needed as food for animals, and the Minister of Food wrote that month: "I wish to make an appeal for the immediate help of every man, woman and child in my effort to reduce the consumption of bread. We must all eat less food; especially we must all eat less bread and none of it must be wasted."

The shortages meant food in transit to the schools was frequently stolen and there was a break-in at the poultry farm in January 1918 when 30 fowls were stolen.

By the spring of 1918 children in the Home came from 12 different poor law unions. There were 576 children on 13 July 1918, but 234 of them, in 13 cottages, were isolated due to an epidemic of mumps. Pupil numbers reached 624 by 1919.

For the signing of the armistice on 11 November 1918, patriotic songs were sung from 11.30 to 12.00, and pupils had a half day off. Everything had become second rate due to shortages during the war. For example, the vast size of the site meant children had to walk a long way, sometimes in bad weather, but one day in February 1919, the Headmaster recorded: "The path and road were in a terrible condition...Many of the older scholars were sent to their respective cottages with stockings and boots saturated with the slush. The quality of the leather now used, even in brand new boots, was powerless to prevent the feet from getting wet."

The whole country was expected to make do, and a competition was held by the *Daily News* for children to produce the most useful items from domestic rubbish. In the carpentry, plumbing and metal workshops, boys produced gas ring kettles, oil lamps, saucepans and so on from tin cans and other waste. Boys from Shirley won five out of 17 top prizes. George Hunt, 15, won £1 for a Coal Hod and Lining; others received ten shillings.

The 32 housemothers at Shirley Schools, sent a petition for a war bonus. Their salary was £34 a year, from which £1 17s 8d was deducted for superannuation, but was only worth half its value owing to the war conditions. The Housemothers could not understand the reluctance of the board for their claim for increased remuneration and felt that the Guardians did not appreciate their services and the matter was referred to the Finance Committee.

In 1918 there were proposals for staff to be limited to a 48 hour working week. However, this would be impossible to manage since the housemothers were supposed to be in the role of surrogate mothers. The Headmaster wrote that to introduce another mother, or two, to cover for the main mother, "would interfere materially with the home life of the children and would consequently destroy the perception and spirit in which the Home was first inaugurated". There was no easy way out of this problem and eventually the Headmaster's suggested compromise solution was accepted by the Guardians: that the mothers would be on duty $71\frac{1}{2}$ hours, the additional time to be paid as overtime, so they would receive £45 per year.

Following the Education Act of 1918, the Poor Law schools were being brought into line with the London County Council schools. In terms of pay, this was very welcome. In 1918 the Headmaster was receiving £300 per year, which was to rise by £25 increments annually. Assistant School Master Ernest Small received £200, while Assistant School Mistress Annie Boots, had £150.

In 1919 the School Committee met to consider the suggestion of a grant of £25 to the Headmaster for his services during the Great War. He had dealt with 24 changes of staff at his offices, and had great problems in obtaining supplies. One member asked if there had been any discrepancies in the books of the School during the period, and was told that a total of £19 could not be accounted for due to the books having been removed from the office for audit. For some considerable time, entries had to be recorded on slips of paper, some of which had been lost. However, there had been no money taken.

Two members of Guardians felt that a slur was being cast on the Headmaster's good name and expressed regrets at one member's line of questioning, saying: "there isn't a finer institution in the whole world than the school." They suggested that the Headmaster should be offered £50 rather than a mere £25. By six votes to four, the Board declined this amendment, but the £25 was awarded.

The Great War was not forgotten. In 1920 an official from the League of Nations gave a lantern slide lecture show at Shirley which included "many interesting pictures of the ravages of war."

Health Between the Wars

The immediate post-war period began with the massive influenza epidemic of 1918, when thousands died across the country. Over 300 children and a large number of staff were ill with the virus at Shirley Schools, but they all recovered, with the exception of one girl who developed complications and died.

The major illnesses were diphtheria, rheumatic fever, mumps, scarlet fever, measles, German measles, chicken pox and whooping cough. The control of infectious diseases is the ever-present theme of the Medical Officer Dr Ridley's monthly reports. Children were frequently referred for an operation for removal of the tonsils and adenoids, which could cause problems if they became infected and turned septic. The Medical Officer noted on 27 April 1920: "On going through the School a few days [ago], I noticed that some of the classrooms were over-crowded and the atmosphere of the rooms was not what it should be. This is a condition which is a common cause of Tonsilitis [sic], of which we have got a very large amount here."

Examinations of tonsils and adenoids to diagnose who needed operations were performed under chloroform after the administration by syringe of a small amount of atrophia to relax the throat muscles. For these operations, Dr Ridley requested a fee of 10s 6d per case. It must have netted him a tidy sum, as 14 children underwent the procedure on 26 March 1927, and 11 on 6 May.

The Medical Officer would perform the operation himself, with the dentist acting as anaesthetist and administering gas. Dr Ridley remarked that in former times he did not ask for payment but "today, we live under different conditions", and he proposed a fee

Laundry on the left of the swimming pool, which fronts the massive water tower (a local landmark) which was occupied by the War Office during the First World War. Photographed in September 1929.

of £1 a case, to be divided between himself and the dentist.

The Medical Officer also looked after the staff. A report of 4 January 1921 reads: "Miss Shaw, Housemother, has been off duty for five weeks in the Infirmary, suffering with "Melancholia and fits of depression". It ws a common complaint. A few weeks later, on 25 January, it was reported that Miss Hawley,

another housemother, had been off duty for three weeks with "general debility", and a Miss Dunt was off duty with "general debility and mental depression". By 15 February, Dr Ridley suggested that these three, and a housekeeper called Miss M. Adlam, had "become incapable of discharging the duties of their respective offices with efficiency, by reason of permanent infirmity of mind or body".

THE SOUTHWARK AND BERMONDSEY RECORDER AND SOUTH LONDON GAZETTE.

FRIDAY, JANUARY 18th, 1928.

Southwark & Bermondsey Recorder AND South London Gazette.

Neutral in Politics. Undenominational.

DIPHTHERIA RAMPANT IN SHIRLEY SCHOOLS.

BERMONDSEY GUARDIANS APPEAL TO CROYDON FOR HELP.

Diphtheria, we understand, is rampant at the Bermondsey Board of Guardians' Schools at Shirley, and as the outbreak is very serious, the Guardians have sent an S.O.S. to Croydon in the following terms: —"That the Croydon County Borough Council be asked whether they would permit the Medical Officer of Health of Croydon to assist the Guardians in attempting to stop the outbreak of diphtheria at the Schools, and the recurrence thereof, by making arrangements for the Schick test to be put into practice at the Schools, followed by inoculation of those found by such test to be susceptible to diphtheria, and that the Guardians would be willing to defray the cost as agreed between the two Boards.

" Before any action is taken to apply the Schick test or inoculation to any of the children of the schools, the parents' consent is to be obtained."

" The Schick Test," says the Schools' Committee, in a report to the Guardians, "consist of the injection into the skin of the persons to be treated of a minute quantity of diphtheria toxin—a positive reaction is shown by the occurrence of a roughly circular area of redness around the site of the injection, and only occurs in those not naturally immune to diphtheria; the test is quickly and practically painlessly carried out with no serious after effects at all, and only extremely seldom does a child ever feel poorly for a day after it; as soon as a child has been proved to be non-immune, it is forthwith immunised, which is carried out by the injection of a small amount of diphtheria toxin largely neutralised by antitoxin; three such doses have generally proved sufficient; that the children would be able to pursue their educational studies and also be able to participate in their usual recreations."

In some quarters, we should add, the Schick Test is severely criticised, and opposed with as much vigour as is vaccination.

A major illness at Shirley, diphtheria was highlighted in this article in 1928

Sometimes the staff were responsible for illness. On 21 June 1921 William Potter, a Bandboy, was reported to have been admitted to the Infirmary "suffering from wheals over the back of his body from his having been thrashed by the Bandmaster".

Sad events happened in this era before antibiotics, when a simple scratch could have terrible consequences. Nine year old Elizabeth Burgess was on the Shirley Hills on 11 August 1922, when a branch of a bramble bush struck her across the face. Her eye became inflamed, then infected, and in three days "acute suppuration had set in" and the eye had to be removed.

One girl, eleven year old Charlotte Bennett, had been in the school's infirmary for four months suffering from heart disease following tonsillitis and rheumatism. When she appeared to be getting worse, Dr Ridley reported on 17 June 1924 that he had her sent to the Poor Law Infirmary, not wanting her to die in the school, "as a death here produces such a period of gloom and depression on the children".

The Medical Officer was particularly concerned about infectious diseases entering the closed community of the schools. On 22 September 1925 he reported how two cases of scarlet fever occurred in one of the cottages after they had been free from infectious disease for ten weeks. This followed a time when, owing to bad weather, the children were kept in and spent time looking at books sent by Bermondsey Public Library. It was the custom of the library to send 'condemned' books, to be taken out of circulation, to Shirley. Dr Ridley said the books "are none too clean and often filthy dirty, and may be carriers of disease of an infectious nature. If these books are no longer fit to be in circulation in the homes of Bermondsey, they are certainly not in a fit state for use in these schools."

The Medical Officer was also responsible for the children's diet, and sometimes, as on 22 June 1922, had to report that he had condemned kitchen supplies – in this case three lots of bread, on three consecutive days – "as being unfit for food".

He was also concerned about conditions caused by the coldness of the cottages in winter. A report of 5 March 1929 remarks on the large number of children in the infirmary with 'broken chilblains' and 'chapped hands'. The Medical Officer advised that "warmer stockings or two pairs should be worn by children known to be susceptible to chilblains". 'Chapped hands' were thought to be caused by children washing in water which was too cold, or failing to dry their hands sufficiently.

Fashionable remedies also intruded into Shirley Schools. Dr Ridley, sounding suspiciously like a sales brochure, reported on 7 May 1927: "Sunlight has the greatest healing power on the earth. This is entirely due to the Ultra Violet Rays. An ordinary window shuts off these rays, but science has stepped in and discovered a new window glass which allows these rays to pass through. With this glass in the windows, health rays flood rooms every hour of clear daylight. It is now being largely used in many institutions. Every school, nursery and infirmary should use this glass. It is the invention of Mr F. E. Lamplough, MA, Fellow of Trinity College, Cambridge."

Dr Ridley left Shirley Schools at the end of 1927. His successor, Dr Jones, had no such faith in the beneficial properties of Vita Glass, but advised the installation of an ultra-violet lamp in the infirmary. He wrote on 10 January 1928 that it "could be used for specific treatment of all convalescent patients before discharge from the Infirmary". A sister was sent to the Electro-therapeutical Department of Croydon General Hospital for instruction in use of the lamp. It proved successful: on 9 October 1928, it was reported that: "the Artificial Sunlight Treatment Centre is in full swing. Twenty-three children are receiving treatment with most gratifying results."

The 1920s

In the latter part of 1920, due to an impending coal strike, the Minister of Health had instructed all public institutions to buy extra reserves of coal. The Headmaster duly ordered an additional 103 tons. In doing so, however, he incurred the displeasure of the contract committee for acting "without the sanction and the authority of the Guardians, who wanted him suspended from duty pending the outcome of an enquiry by the Minister of Health". However, one level-headed member of the Committee made the point that if there had been an "excess zest" on the part of the Headmaster, it was in the interest of the children. The matter was not pursued.

In February 1923 a troop of Boy Scouts consisting of 48 lads between 11 and 14 years old was organised, to be known as '32 of Croydon Shirley Troop of Boy Scouts'. They would receive training in first-aid, signalling, pioneering, map reading and drawing, woodcraft, camp cookery, knot tying and compass reading.

December 1923 saw the Schools Committee giving weighty consideration to the possibility of installing a wireless at the school. After much deliberation they came to the conclusion that it would be "a most useful form of training and amusement" and unanimously authorised the total expenditure of £27.16 for the purchase and delivery of a complete set of wireless aerial equipment.

The 1920s were the high point of development for Shirley Schools. Now they had a strong tradition to draw on and a pride in previous achievements. J.Chuter Ede, Secretary to the National Union of Teachers, visited the school, and wrote on 18 June 1920: "I was highly impressed by the free atmosphere that pervaded the whole school. The manner in which to these children of hopeless heredity a stimulating esprit de corps has been given was an inspiration." He was particularly pleased to hear that of all the boys who had been sent to service, only one had later become chargeable under the Poor Law (presumably by being sent to the workhouse). The Headmaster reconfirmed this and added that the failure of the placement was due to the influence of an uncle. One girl had similarly become chargeable in all the time the school had been opened, and she was said to be "mentally deficient".

It was a good record but, of course, was achieved by discarding the most intractable children by sending them back to the workhouse or to another institution before they reached an age when they would be sent to service.

In the spring of 1920 the Guardians of Godstone and Westbourn asked for accommodation for some of their boys at a rate of 19s 3d a week. Since it was much cheaper to have a full complement of children at the school, this was agreed to. However, it was pointed out that children from Bermondsey should always have first claim on the school in every way.

The *Croydon Advertiser* reported the school sports day in June 1920: "All was sunshine and blue sky, smiles and laughter, mirth and lively, innocent abandonment to natural, healthy impulses. The creeper-clad houses, placed at all angles, in the very pink of neatness and good order, with nodding hollyhocks, climbing roses and hosts of other summer flowers combining to banish every suggestion of that hateful word 'institution', struck visitors with renewed pleasure. In these houses, with their see-saws and swings and broad, grassy, open spaces around, there trooped eager, expectant children to the cricket field for a programme of well over 30 athletic events. Boots and clothes that anyone would wear, all made by the boys, are to be seen. The girls had on show cooking which would please the palate of the most fastidious, and dresses which would be in place in the West End."

"One particularly noticed the practical education given to the boys in doing household-repairs of all kinds, and producing household requisites – even a coal box and shovel from packing case wood and pail handle and a saucepan handle. There were gas shades made out of old beef tins and wire tongs for taking eggs out of boiling water. Even miniature aquariums are constructed."

In 1920 too, perhaps for the first time, Shirley Schools children won scholarships to continue their education beyond elementary level: three boys to John Ruskin School, and two girls to Lady Edridge. In 1921, 13 boys entered for the certificate in Pitman's Shorthand, with 12 gaining the certificate.

Children were increasingly involved with activities outside the schools, like the Girl Guides of whom there were 50 members, all of them winning the Folk Song and Dance Badge, "designed to interest the present generation in the songs, dances and customs of Merrie England". Thirty girls went camping to Addington.

The School Committee agreed, in October 1920, to reimburse 8s 6d to Mr J. F. H. Roberts, to replace the cost of his glasses. He had an accident while on business driving his rally car to Croydon. The cob slipped on some very smooth stone and tripped his cart up, throwing him out on his head. His pince-nez were run over by a motor bus.

In 1921 Shirley entered the Excelsior League, competing in games with – and winning against – non-Poor Law schools. That same year, Shirley School boys won the Westminster Challenge Cup. They beat Hanwell 4–1, after trailing 1–0 at half time. In 1930 they made the front page of the *Southwark & Bermondsey Recorder, and South London Gazette* newspaper after winning through to the final of the same competition.

Sport was not the only news item reported locally. The following article was included in the same newspaper on 3 March 1922.

The School's Committee reported that they had given instructions for 134 tins of potted lobster to be destroyed as unfit for food. It was part of a consignment bought in June 1917.

Another off-beat article that was featured in the *Manchester Guardian* on 27 November 1922 is reprinted below.

"PRETTY POLLY'S RATIONS"
SENSATION OVER ITEM IN GUARDIANS'
ACCOUNT: SHOCK FOR AUDITORS.

You who sometimes doubt whether our Civil Servants earn their money, listen to the sad story of the Bermondsey Poll Parrot, and the tremendous commotion it caused in Whitehall.

In the beginning the Head Master of the Shirley Schools, which belong to the Bermondsey Guardians, bought a parrot for the amusement of the children in his care. A nice, ladylike parrot it was, free from vice, and with a vocabulary as innocuous as the babbling of a new born babe.

Once, during the General Election ,it was heard to whisper a fear that its food would cost it more, but that was the only time it fell from grace.

One day someone sent out some food from the parrot's larder; the usual mixture of bird seed, monkey nuts and broken biscuits. And through an oversight the two shillings thus spent was recorded in the school accounts.

Presently there arrived on the premises the Board of Health auditor and the corps of eagle-eyed clerks; and, with noses trained to smell out scandals, bribery and corruption, they swooped hawklike upon that innocent two bob, demanding explanations.

The Ministry was informed, and in solemn conclave they sat them down to consider the position.

"Parrot's food! And do children, may I ask, eat parrot's food? Is it rich in vitamins? Is it sustaining and nourishing, and full of beans? "It was explained that the parrot's food was for the school parrot who was not on the strength.

"Good Heavens! said the Board of Health. "Do my ears deceive me, or can such things really be? A parrot indeed! And is it, may we ask, a

nationalised parrot, a municipal parrot, or a privately-owned bird?"

"But there is no precedent for this thing," they said. "It can't be done. This is pure simony or something." And they wrote to the Bermondsey Guardians demanding an explanation on form B. 763/22 with several carbon copies.

"And the Board of Guardians told the Clerk to the Board of Guardians, and the Clerk to the Board of Guardians wrote to the head master demanding, in turn, several more explanations, with any amount of carbon copies, each in duplicate.

In due course the head master informed the clerk that it was all a mistake, that he paid for the parrot's keep out of his own pocket, the entry being an oversight.

So the Clerk wrote to the Guardians, and the Guardians ordered the papers to be placed on the table, and moved that the head master be referred back, and filed for reference, and brought to the notice of the proper authorities, nem. con., ad lib., and sin die. to add to its number, and anything may happen at any moment, if not sooner.
Meanwhile

> *The Parrot still is sitting,*
> *Never flitting, never flitting*
> *From his perch inside the sitting*
> *room upon the second floor.*
> *And his eyes are ever blinking*
> *Mostly blinking, sometimes winking,*
> *Just as if he had been drinking*
> *Rather hard the night before.*
> *Not a single word he utters,*
> *But he's thinking all the more.*

A rumour that the bird has suddenly started swearing is officially denied; but no doubt he would if he knew how.

Christmas 1922 was a lavish affair, with the children's own entertainment show, a show by a professional group called 'The Key Koncert Kompanie'; a Punch and Judy Show; a 'Cinematograph' Show; and all the children over six went to the Hippodrome Picture Palace in Church Street, Croydon.

Enterainments became somewhat more sophisticated in the 1920s, with children being given "wireless lectures" where the school wireless apparatus was hooked up to a loudspeaker. Some film was taken of the School itself by Bermondsey Borough Public Health Department, and it was shown in the School hall on 24 September 1929.

In March 1924 the Schools Committee recommended that all children of the age of 12 and above should visit the British Empire Exhibition at Wembley at a cost of 9d per head and 2s 6d for each accompanying teacher.

The Committee reported that at the 1925 Cookery Exhibition at Olympia, the following girls distinguished themselves in the competition for juniors, aged 12–16 years: *Ena Fawdon* – 1st Prize, Silver Medal for a portable dinner for the working man, packed ready to carry. *Lily Newing* – 2nd Prize, Bronze Medal for artisan meal for four people. *Lucy Camp* – Bronze Medal. *Vera Voss* – Diploma. These girls were trained at the Girls' Training Centre under the tuition of Miss Ferguson, cookery and housewifery mistress at Shirley Schools.

It was agreed that the prizes should be presented to the girls at a meeting of the Board. Winning such prizes was something unique in the history of the Schools at Shirley. The working man's dinner, cooked by Miss Fawdon, comprised a meat pudding, cabbage and potatoes, and apple tart.

In March 1929 another cookery exhibition enabled the Chairman, Mr W. J. Craigie, JP, to present medals won at another cookery exhibition by girls of Shirley Schools, and compliment Miss Ferguson on the way in which she trained them. Mr Craigie also presented a bronze medal and a diploma won by two girls in a team competition promoted by the Red Cross Society. He remarked to laughter and applause that the girls who had won medals for cooking a dinner suitable for a working-man would, doubtless, make good little wives when they came to get married.

The Minister of Health (who presumably was involved because of the fear of the spread of infectious diseases) wrote stating that he offered no objection to the proposal of the Guardians to incur reasonable expenditure in permitting the Shirley School Troop of Boy Scouts to attend camp at Eastbourne during the forthcoming summer.

All children in the schools of nine years of age and upwards, were permitted to take part in a children's summer camp at the seaside for 14 days, together with the necessary staff at an approximate net cost of £400, subject to the Minister of Health's sanction.

A deputation visited and inspected the arrangements in force at Dymchurch Holiday Camp, near Folkestone, with a view to ascertain whether the camp was suitable for children from the Schools.

The Farm
At the beginning of the 1920s Shirley had a farm comprising a vegetable garden, pigs, poultry and rabbits. There were eight acres of arable land. The school authorities said that the principal function of the farm was to educate the children in farm work. Moreover, the farm was expected to contribute in kind to the running of the Home: food produced on the farm would save money on Shirley's overall food bill, and so would lead to a positive annual account. The farm supplied poulty and eggs to the Bermondsey and Rotherhithe Hospital, by approval of the Guardians.

In 1921 the district auditor, an official who oversees the spending of public money, produced a very negative report on the farm and the way its finances were reported in Shirley's accounts. The auditor said the accounts showed a large profit of over £268, where in fact, according to proper accounting methods, the farm made a loss over the half year period which was studied.

The auditor accused the Headmaster of an accounting trick to make the figures look better: all of the general overheads for the farm were carried on the general budget and so were the wages of farm staff, amounting to more than £809 for the half year. At least some of these costs should have shown up in the farm's accounts. The auditor wrote about the farm: "There seems little justification for the subsidising of an enterprise which, whilst showing a 'paper' profit, actually involves an appreciable loss in the working". The Head-master argued that it was not a commercial farm but mainly educational. The auditor noted that boys worked without pay on the farm, as part of their training. He noted that the accounts also failed to show, on the debit side, depreciation on implements and utensils which would ultimately have to be replaced.

A more stringent criticism was of the running of the farm itself, which was said to be unprofitable because it was so inefficient. The auditor remarked: "Pigs should be a source of profit at an institution maintaining about 600 children, where the swill should be considerable. Breeding is undertaken, but there were only four litters during the half year...The supply of eggs seems remarkably poor. Between 5 October and 6 December, 19 hens and about 45 pullets between them produced no more than four."

The Bermondsey Guardians accepted the main points of the report and ordered new accounting methods along the lines recom-mended by the district auditor. They gave a defence of the general running of the farm, however, remarking that the pigs had been unprofitable only in the half year examined by the auditor, and that was because both their own boar and a boar borrowed from a neighbouring farm were partially or wholly impotent, so few piglets were produced. For the corresponding period in 1920, under better circumstances, 215 piglets were produced. Likewise, the district auditor had studied the hens at a period when they were in moult, a time when few poultry farmers have a good yield.

By the summer of 1925, the Schools Committee recommended to substitute butter for margarine for all children in the Home. The national newspaper, *The Daily Herald*, printed an article, dated 9 March 1927, about life at the Bermondsey Guardians School at Shirley:

MRS LONDON AND HER MANY CHILDREN

A visitor from Moscow was recently shown round the Bermondsey Guardians' School at Shirley. He grew more and more bewildered. At last (the Headmaster told me) he stopped and said: "It is very strange. I took all my ideas of your Poor Law system from the works of your writer, Charles Dickens, and this (he threw out his arms expressively) is so different."

I could well understand. Shirley is a surprising place. Although an 'institution', it gives the impression of a beautiful English village, with an uncommon share of green spaces. The 38 cottage homes are spread along two miles of roads.

There are elementary schools, and technical schools completely equipped for the training of boys in carpentry, engineering, plumbing, tailoring, boot-making, bandsmanship, gardening, agriculture; and of girls in dress-making, laundry work, cooking, and all the arts of the housewife. There are playing-fields, a model farm, a gymnasium, and a swimming-bath. Oliver Twist could not have asked for more.

It is some comfort for those who believe in progress, to recall that 'Oliver Twist' was written in the first years of Victoria, and that in the Bermondsey Guardians were building Shirley. They did it in this spirit. When they bought these

Gardening and farming were established activities from early on as this 1907 picture shows

75 acres, they said: "We will have none of your institutional uniformity. We will shake a 38 dice out of a box onto a map, and where they fall, we will build our cottages."

It couldn't be done quite like that, but it was very nearly; and the only likeness I could trace with Bumble was the alphabetical christening of the cottages: Acacia, Ash, Beech, Birch, Bramble and so on. (Bumble, you remember, on the same system named his 'foundlings' Swubble, Twist, Unwin, Vilkins.)

Traversing half the alphabet and passing through the Stores, where boys were sorting provisions into parcels for cottages, I found the Headmaster in an inner room, and was rather alarmed to hear that "the Board was sitting in solemn conclave", and I was to have the honour to go around in their company.

However, the party dwindled to four. There was the clergyman, whose roving eye found the blackbird half-completed nest in the hedge near the band-room; he was an idealist and full of schemes. The Headmaster, of inventive brain and even temperament, talked of feeding troughs and football matches, of Cox's Orange Pippins and see-saws: from time to time he pointed out practical objections to the reverend gentleman's proposals.

The Chairman said little but, at the height of discussion, his left eye would slowly close and as slowly re-open, an eloquent spot in an otherwise solemn countenance. It was pleasant to see how the small children ran to greet these gentlemen; but embarrassing when I was the last to leave a classroom of five-year-olds, to be in the full fire of a salvo of kisses blown from forty pairs of shameless lips. The older children were well-spoken, answering questions sensibly, not in the least shy.

"We have 608" said the Headmaster, "evenly divided between the sexes. We take them from $11\frac{1}{2}$ to 16. The population of Bermondsey has dwindled so much that more than half are now boarders from other places. We charge includes education, and make a profit." (Oliver's foster-mother, you remember, charged $7\frac{1}{2}$d and also made a profit.)

The elementary schools are on the London County County lines, and several boys a year win scholarships to the Croydon secondary schools. The training in the technical schools is thorough. I saw a young plumber who had seen to what was wrong in one of the cottages, had located the defect, and written his report in lucid English, and was now carrying out a repair in a workmanlike fashion.

A tailor of 15, sitting cross-legged and already acquiring the gravity of the trade, showed me the waistcoat he was making, and told me he had graduated through trousers, and was yet to advance to jackets. ("We have old boys as cutters earning £700 a year" said the Headmaster.) All the clothes for the children are made in the schools, and so are the boots.

At band practice were learners stiffened by a few men, like the ruddy lad who had come from the farm to play the enormous B flat tuba. Small boys favoured the cornet: not so very big a boy, the trombone. They played a foxtrot and the R.A. quick march in almost professional style, and I was not surprised to hear that the band had a famous reputation.

About the farm, I would say only this. If you think pigs must needs be dirty creatures, see those at Shirley. Environment counts!

The cottages would lower the pride of a Dutch housewife. The floors have never known soap; they are polished like a mirror. The stairs are of teak; the walls distempered in pleasant colours; there are books, pictures; games: each child has a locker for his own treasures. We found babies at tea: so far from asking their foster mother for more, they offered us bites of their bread and butter.

"I wish you could see some of the 'homes' they come from", said the clergyman. He told me of one block of dwellings owned by a great public company - and of other things. Shirley is building a new generation out of an old.

Clouds? Two. So many young children had recently been taken - "False economy" said the clergyman. "I was always against it", that the technical shops are not getting all the big boys they could take. And London's suburbs are creeping up to the boundary fence. The purchase of a small piece of land would keep backyards at arm's length: the whole place is so big, an argument for the wide and generous outlook that surely this will be managed.

"Some day", said the Headmaster, "when the Guardians cease to need Shirley, London will take it over as a fully-equipped technical and agricultural school, ready to her hand. Such another place will never be seen. For one thing, the cost of building it now would be four times as great." "And the rest", said the Chairman.

Three orphaned lads, aged 16, brought up in Shirley Schools, and recently sent to work for Mr R. Mansell, Building Contractor, in Croydon, attended a meeting in January 1925 before the Board of Guardians. It was proposed in the presence of Mr Mansell, that these lads should be apprenticed for five pounds a year, at a wage of £1 per week, increasing by 5s per week each year. The boys spoke to the Guardians saying they "liked their job and were comfortably lodged".

Mr Mansell explained that the boys were very attentive to their duties and, as yet, had never had a bad boy from the Schools. Twenty had passed through his employment, and one of them, who had been with him for a long decade, was now second in charge. Mr Mansell continued to say that the three lads before the Guardians could not be made to understand that they ought to attend technical classes in the evening. The boys, after being questioned individually by the Chairman, stated that they would be prepared to attend workshops at least two nights a week. The Board resolved that such attendance should be made obligatory in the indentures that were signed after the meeting.

Pupils benefited from a new attitude towards work and remuneration. From January 1926, children in industrial training received a shilling a week.

Dress was unchanged, except that the Matron, Miss F. E. Capes, arranged for girls to wear a 'liberty bodice' in 1926, in place of a corset, as "girls object to wearing corsets and they are not durable".

A new block was added in 1926 for the training of 30 older girls preparing for domestic services. An extension was built onto the infirmary enabling it to accommodate 48 patients, an increase of 24 beds.

An article from *The Bromley Mercury* dated 1 June 1928:

SHIRLEY SCHOOLS VISITED BY BROMLEY DICKENSIANS

A model institution of its kind, Shirley Homes, the School of the Bermondsey Guardians, was visited, on Saturday, by a party of 20 members and friends of the Bromley branch of the Dickens Fellowship. Situated amid delightful surroundings in Wickham road, Shirley, the school covers an area of 78 acres. As one saunters through the grounds, the roads and footpaths which traverse them make it difficult to realise one is on enclosed premises. An air of cleanliness and healthiness pervades the place and is especially noticeable in the neat little cottages where the children live. These cottages are found at regular intervals and have large airy rooms. Each cottage has a bathroom.

The children themselves look the picture of health, and a pleasing feature one noticed was the absence of uniformity about their dress. Environment is said to play a great part in the formation of character, and children raised in the atmosphere of Shirley Schools cannot fail to become good citizens, especially those who are brought there as babies. Children are taken from the age of three months and school life ends at 14.

The Dickensians visited the well equipped school, similar to an ordinary elementary school, but possessing a very fine hall. The hall was original designed as a chapel, but never has been consecrated.

The school has a very fine band, which is much in demand for garden parties, etc. The band earns an average of £80 a year, part of which is divided amongst the members of the band.

Shirley's Sports Day 1928

A reporter from the *Southwark Recorder* dated 20 July 1928 described the open day that summer:

"SUNNY REVELS AT SHIRLEY"
SPORTS FESTIVAL AT
BERMONDSEY POOR LAW SCHOOLS
Ministry of Health Inspector Looks On.

"This magnificent school, Shirley, makes every arrangement for sport and games to be carried out in public school spirit, and the greatest importance is attached to this school training." No truer words were ever uttered, nor could their truth have been more successfully and pleasurably demonstrated than was done on Saturday. It is not often that the parents and friends of the scholars have such a gloriously fine day for witnessing this important festival. The sun shone with its old time brilliance (after two years seclusion), from a cloudless sky, and the air was so clear that the visitors on the sports ground had a magnificent, far-reaching panoramic view of the neighbouring country, with the Crystal Palace looking astonishingly near, as a central feature. There must have been something like a record attendance of visitors – 2,000 probably, and despite the heat, no-one appeared anxious to get away until the proceedings ended.

Among the spectators was Mr Blight, Assistant Inspector, who expressed his personal pleasure of the sports competitors, and the excellent part singing by the school choir. There were so many well-known people, that we could only mention a

Ash and Acacia Cottages covered with ivy, September 1929

few. The Mayor and Mayoress of Bermondsey (Alderman and Mrs Balman), Mrs Drapper (Mayor of Deptford), were among them, together with members of the Schools Committee.

For the sports, with the day's doings commenced, the Guardians had been given permission by the Ministry to spend a maximum of £25 in prizes, and these, together with the number of magnificent challenge shields and cups, made a glittering display on the table near the centre of the course, close to the band enclosure. Above the field, fluttering gaily from the ropes and poles, was a lavish display of bunting, among which appeared the flags of different Nations.

The competitors in the numerous events showed the utmost enthusiasm, despite the hot weather, but perhaps the most popular event of all was "tilting the bucket", the consequence of which at almost every individual effect was a thorough drenching with cold water for the competitors.

Another amusing event was the tug-of-war between boys and girls. The girls easily won – but for the sake of the boys prestige, we hasten to add that there were ten girls – all of them hefty – on the rope and only eight boys, hardly one of whom was as big as their fair opponents. In the old scholars' race, Mr J T Hunt, an old Shirley schoolboy, and now one of the Bermondsey Guardians, was a competitor. Very pretty were the Maypole dancers by infant boys and girls, and the dancing display that followed was both graceful and spectacular. A company of lithe, well-built boys, under the direction of their instructor, Sergeant Coombes, gave a gymnastics and physical drill display which could not have been improved upon, and like the dancers who preceded them, they received quite an ovation from the spectators at the close of their performance.

After tea, the schools brass band, whose high reputation is widely known, played well-diversified selections, Mr Evens Parr, A.L.C.M. (late 1st Life Guards) conducting. The items included well-known and difficult selections by Schumann, Sullivan and Verdi. Tubular bell effects went particularly well.

The schools choir took the field, giving several items from their repertoire. It was most melodious unaccompanied singing, for which they received tremendous applause, showing apparently that they are as popular even as the band.

Early in the evening, Mr Craigie distributed the prizes won in the sports and school competitions, among the latter being honours awards as follows, for the best boys and girls:

Day school scholars, Jessie Northey, James Tyrrell. Evening Continuation School scholars, Alice Pearson, Charles Hogben. Domestic Servant, Maud Reynolds, Cricketer, season 1928 footballer, season 1927-28, Albert Moggeridge. Swimmers Edna West, Chas. Habgood. Gymnast, Sammual Rapley. Band Sergeant, William Tumnor. Certificates awarded for Proficiency in Shorthand (awarded by Pitman's Commercial College): E Phillips, D Dilon, S Kircher, J Rolfe, A Moggeridge, C. Hogben.

Mr Small, the Headmaster, in asking Mr Craigie to distribute the prizes, said he had the whole of the staff heartily backing him up, and making this annual festival the great success it was, and wished to thank everybody who was co-operating with him in any way with that object in view. The speaker specially mentioned, among others, the band and the choir, of which latter Mr Buckingham is the conductor. Mr Small said they received letters from all over the world from boys who had sang in the Shirley Schools Choir. These boys and girls wanted to know how the choir was going on, and sometimes wished to know what songs they were singing nowadays. He had been asked whether the services of the choir would be utilised this day at the sports! It was quite unthinkable that the sports would ever be held without them (applause).

With regard to the dances, he thought his hearers would have to go a long way to see anything as good (applause). It was all part of the plan to brighten up the lives of the Shirley Schools children with music, dancing and gymnastics (applause). The speaker mentioned that the swimming sports day would be held in September.

Games and Recreations for Children— Training of.

◎ ◎

The following is a copy of a Report received from Mr. C. F. Roundell, Inspector of the Ministry of Health, and made by Mr. Noel Curtis Bennett after a visit to the Schools, relative to facilities for games and recreation for children as follows :—

BERMONDSEY SCHOOLS AT SHIRLEY.

This magnificent school makes every arrangement for sport and games to be carried out in a public school spirit, and the greatest importance is attached to this side of the school training. There are large and open grounds for football, cricket, hockey and netball, and in addition there are several Long Jumps, High Jumps, Swings, &c., throughout the grounds, where the children are encouraged to take exercise when not in school. The school takes part in the competitions organised by the Poor Law Schools Athletic Association, and matches are also played against good local schools and Clubs. They hold Annual Sports each year, which the Headmaster tells me are most elaborately carried out, and create great enthusiasm. Inter-school competitions take place in all forms of sport, and for this purpose the Houses are grouped and called after the name of a famous Club or County. For instance, in cricket " Kent play Surrey." In football " Tottenham Hotspur play Aston Villa," and the boys wear the colours of the Club on their arms. This produces a very great keenness on the part of the boys and the greatest rivalry exists. The school is fortunate in having a large number of magnificent trophies, and each year awards Honours for the best cricketer, footballer, swimmer, &c., on the same lines as scholars. Each boy or girl in the school has half-an-hour physical training a day and the tone and esprit-de-corps of the school is excellent.

Extract from the programme of the 26th Annual Inspection and Sports, Saturday 13 July 1929

They had to thank a number of people for voluntary services in connection with last year's swimming sports, the boy scouts and girl guide movements and the cultivation of allotments, and also to thank the donors of prizes, including Miss Walmsley, of the Ministry of Health, and an old boy who had given a prize for the most popular boy in the Schools (applause).

Mr Craigie, in a characteristically humorous speech, addressed mainly to the children, said that this was a record gathering, which showed that his hearers took as great an interest in the Schools as the Guardians did. Because the outside people were interested, the Guardians were all the more anxious that the schools should be a great success. He pointed out that the attendance of guests was so large on this occasion that it would be impossible to feed the two thousand, for the tea contractor had not expected half that number.

The speaker also mentioned that a new doctor had been appointed for the Schools, but judging by the look of the children, he said, there was not much need for his services at the moment (laughter). They also had a new board of Guardians, but it was guaranteed only for three years (laughter).

He wondered what would happen if the Guardians lost control of the Schools. However, they were determined to continue meanwhile, as in the past, to look after the needs and welfare of every boy and girl in the Schools, quite irrespective, he remarked, of whether the children belonged to Bermondsey or some district. Under no circum-stances were they going to see any deterioration in the standard now existing in those Schools, under which standard every boy and girl was given a fair chance in life (applause) - a better chance than many of the older people present had in their youth. Everyone present would agree, regardless of politics, that the Bermondsey Board of Guardians were doing their utmost to train children in the way they should go, and doing their utmost in every way, so that all the children might grow up to be useful citizens who could look after themselves and be a credit to the country we were

proud of (applause). In 1930 there would be a change in the education system of the whole country. They hoped it would be advantageous to the children, but in any event the Bermondsey Board of Guardians would take steps to make sure that the Shirley Schools were not left behind the times (applause).

The proceedings terminated with votes of thanks and the National Anthem.

Achievements
Shirley Schools pupils continued to achieve in scholarships, music and sports. Florence White, Frederick Tyrrell and William Dunn, all pupils at Shirley Schools, were awarded scholarships to secondary schools in Croydon during 1929. In April of that year the Shirley School Prized Band became the only Poor Law School band to win two certificates and prize money in the Southern Counties Boy's Contest. They were placed second in the March and third in the Overture. George Young won a Gold Medal for being the best trombone player to play in the competition. Four boys from Shirley Schools won the invitation relay race at the Ministry of Health's sports competition at Chiswick on 12 June 1929, an event open to all Metropolian Poor Law Schools.

The End of the Guardians
In 1929 there were 146 staff, of whom 78 were resident. The Home was registered for 680 children and beds were provided for 269 boys and 281 girls, though the number resident in 1929 was 475. The children were mainly from the Bermondsey district, but others came from Poplar, Dartford, Epsom, Richmond, Chertsey and Battle.

Many of the staff were at the Schools a very long time. Miss Wood, Housemother at Violet Cottage, gave 20 years service. Miss Alice Green worked at the Schools for 25 years. It was not uncommon for housemothers to work at Shirley for many years. Mrs Jane Tickel and

Ellen Penrose had been at the Schools since 1904 and stayed 21 years and 18 years respectively.

In 1928 the Headmaster's doctor wrote to the Guardians to say he was "suffering from heart disease of a progressive type, necessitating prolonged rest and freedom from all worry and mental strain". Roberts himself wrote: "I have laboured diligently and with enthusiasm in the past, but my life's work is now ended." He was 59 and retired with a pension of £465 a year. Mrs Roberts, who had worked as his assistant, received £111. His place was taken by Ernest Small.

Administration by the Guardians did not long outlast Roberts. The last meeting of the Schools Committee before everything was handed over to the London County Council, happened on 1 March 1930. In that year 619 children lived at the Schools.

Boys gymnastics group, 1907

Children at Shirley made full use of the swimming facilities and often competed with other schools

CHAPTER THREE

The London County Council

The new managing committee of the Children's Home, Shirley, first met on 26 March 1930, and appointed Mrs Eveline Lowe, JP as Chairman. The establishment was re-named Shirley Residential School.

In 1930 a holiday relief housemother received £1.55 per week plus food and lodging. This can be compared to the wage for a night watchman on the site of £3 8s 6d, or a laundress at £2 10s 0d.

Recreation

The school band had seven engagements between June and August 1930, being paid up to £7 0s 7d. In the early 1930s the band went to Savoy Hill to broadcast on the BBC's popular 'Children's Hour' radio programme.

The children went on outings, including to the Grand Theatre, Croydon. In 1934 a cinema projector and screen were bought so films could be shown in the school. School journeys increased – 40 boys went to Hawkshill Camp in Kent in summer 1935. The Special Services Sub-Committee that year declared that all children over ten would go for a fortnight's holiday under canvas at Dymchurch or Walton-on-the-Naze. Twenty-four girl guides from the Schools (32nd of Croydon) went on a two-week camping holiday at a cost of £70.

The Wickham Road entrance to the school, close to the Shirley Inn c. 1935. The growth of the area is clearly seen when compared with the photograph on page 6.

The games and recreation fund of £190 for 1935-36 included the production of the school magazine, prizes for sports and swimming competitions, books and newspapers, "outings and treats", "maintenance of wireless apparatus and purchase of gramophone records", and "expenses of taking children to cinematographer entertainments". A club room for the elder girls was set up in the girls' training centre.

The management committee, like the Guardians before them, took a keen and close interest in the daily running of the Home. They worried about the weekly allowance of eggs (raised to two per child in 1931) and the length of the grass. There was much discussion over the siting of the girls' and boys' toilets at the summer camp. Fears were expressed that they were positioned too close together "causing anxiety to staff".

A complete survey made numerous recommendations for greater administrative efficiency and improvements, like suggesting children should have a locker outside their bedroom doors and a wicker basket (presumably a large square one) at the foot of their beds. It was agreed that cubicles should be provided for the older girls. Cottage libraries were improved, and three members of staff were given a course in hairdressing so they could improve on the amateur efforts previously made by housemothers on children's hair.

Shirley Residential Schools Staff in formal pose, 1937

Families

The big change in child care between the 1930s and the preceding period was in the attitude of authority to the families of children. It was caused by a change in the attitude to poverty. A positive aspect of the mass unemployment of the 1920s and 1930s was that poverty was no longer seen as simply a moral failing, as it had been in the nineteenth century. This meant that families need not be punished because they were in such miserable circumstances they could not look after their children, nor that families need be feared as a source of moral contagion of their children. Probably this went too far, and children who were in danger of physical abuse were sent back for sojourns with parents.

Friendless Children and Fostering

In the early 1930s, for no reason which appears in the records, administrators of the Home became concerned about 'friendless children' who did not have people outside the institution. A number of means were used to deal with this issue: girls from Bermondsey Central School were encouraged to write letters and send parcels to 'friendless girls' in 1932, though this did not seem to last long.

A conference on friendless children was held, probably in early 1934, for all chairs and vice chairs of managing committee of Homes and all LCC Special Sub-Committee members, and it was agreed that little had been done for 'friendless' children, and action was necessary. It was agreed that "all friendless children considered as suitable should, if possible, be boarded out"; that is, fostered.

A report of 18 July 1934 noted: "Friendless children in the Shirley Residential Schools are being linked up with children in various local schools. Introductions to local families of the artisan class are being arranged." Further arrangements were made in 1935 to provide each friendless boy with an 'uncle' and each friendless girl with an 'aunty'.

The London County Council decided to adapt two empty receiving blocks at the entrance of the Home for children between ars of age. In 1932 the initial reorganisation of Shirley facilities for infants was completed. Now there was accommodation for 100 children under five, of whom 68 were less than three years of age. To ensure proper care for the increase of infants, additional staff would be employed and two full-time housemothers were recruited. The head housemother was

Mealtimes in a girl's cottage 1934; and below, happy faces at a school social and dance, 1937

paid £100 and her deputy £70 a year. Nine junior assistants were also added, receiving £30 in annual wages. Eventually the cost of the wages increased to approximately £440 a year.

An article in the *Croydon Advertiser* in 1933 remarked: "The children are taught cleanliness, order, self-respect and good manners. Endeavour is made to remove all traces of institution life, and consequently a great deal of freedom is allowed. Boys and girls can go to shop or visit Croydon quite freely. It is not the desire of the Council to protect the children too much and thus sap their self-reliance. The children therefore are expected to take ordinary risks like other children. There is a reunion of old scholars each Whit-Monday, and 200 to 250 attend. Records show that the great majority of children sent out from the school become respectable, self-supporting citizens."

During summer 1934, the double cottages Honeysuckle/Hazel and Holly/Heather had a glazed veranda erected costing £329. Babies were accommodated in these cottages. Children had an immunisation programme against scarlet fever.

In 1937, Shirley officials commemorated the coronation of George VI by planting a cedar tree close to the entrance of the Home. The Shirley boys cricket team won a national competition. A trophy was presented by a member of the England team, and the boys were further rewarded by a day out to the Oval.

In 1938 the Children's Committee agreed to a "semi-permanent construction" for use of nursery children. This was built beside Holly/Heather Cottages at a cost of £1 8s 25d. This included lighting and heating by electricity. A glazed veranda ran along the front of the total length of this single floor building. Inside there were three classrooms separated by sliding and folding doors.

Staff preparing for a charabanc outing, September 1937

School

After the LCC took over the school, everything was updated, including the teaching methods. In 1933 the staff were told that "corporal punishment is of little value unless its use is limited". The Headmaster should have discretionary power to cane boys over 14, but must report it in the punishment book.

Sex instruction was first mentioned in 1935, where there was some discussion as to whether the consent of parents was required before children were given such lessons. The management committee asked: "To arrange for the superintendent to warn boys at their final interview before leaving for employment of the impropriety and danger of undue intimacy with boys and men." It was obviously not thought necessary to give a similar warning to girls.

Work

Children were still being 'emigrated', now frequently to Fairbridge Farm School in Western Australia.

The Placing and After-Care Sub-Committee was concerned about the lack of a half-way house for boys who were too old for school, but who had no work. With wage levels based on age, this was an example of how difficult it can be to bring in even an obviously beneficial reform in a localised area. The managing committee decided to deal with each case separately and allow children who wanted to and had the ability to stay until 16. The general school leaving age was not raised to 16 for another 20 years.

There was also concern that boys were being set adrift in the increasingly hostile world of the 1930s, with no obligation on the part of the Home to help. A report read: "We think that in exceptional cases 'after-care' might be continued up to the age of 20, and not cease as at present at the age of 18 years."

Domestic service was still the lot of most girls. They received £18 a year for work as a 'kitchen maid', 'under housemaid' or 'between maid'.

This same committee, reporting on girls in January 1934 remarked: "We have had only one difficult girl to deal with, and she was sent off to one of the MABYS training homes (Scott House in Hitchen). We are reluctant to place girls who are defective (but not certifiable) into domestic service...we do, however, train some difficult girls in our laundry." They considered other work than domestic service, and noted that there had been a few girls in other jobs like the civil service, nursing or waitressing. They also tried putting girls into department stores but the girls left these jobs and went into domestic service as it paid better.

The Second World War

On 24 May 1939 the Headmaster reported on air raid precautions, "including gas proofing of rooms, provision of gas masks for children, blacking out arrangements, and training of decontamination squads". There was a lecture to staff on 11 July 1939 on dealing with a gas attack, the great fear of the early war period. Gas masks were issued to all children in the junior and infant classes on 24 August, and to staff and seniors the following day.

There was a rehearsal for evacuation on 28 August and within days the order was received for evacuation to Maidenhead the next day. So with their personal belongings and their gas masks, the children all went off, presumably to the railway station, to be housed somewhere less likely to be bombed than Shirley. Some school buildings were used as a transit centre and storage depot for emergency equipment.

In 1941-44, part of the school was taken over as a clinic for delinquent girls and a remand home for girls and small boys, which had formerly been at Stamford House, in Shepherd's Bush. A clinic for girls suffering from venereal disease was also opened. When the clinic was first opened, a nursing sister: "expressed the opinion that many of the girls did not realise the seriousness of the disease", so they were shown films on VD. Further lectures and films on sex were authorised for the girls in October 1942.

In order that there was no reflection on Shirley children, the name of the Home was changed to Wickham Road Remand Home. In January 1943 there were 94 children there: 15 of these in the clinic. There had been 259 admissions since the previous meeting, in October, so the turnover was considerable.

In 1943 MABYS notified the London County Council of its intention to discontinue its activities. The LCC assumed its responsibilities, taking over the Association's hostel at 94 Oakley Street, London SW3, known after 1945 as Mavis Hostel. "It was time this narrow tradition was broken. The girls should be encouraged to seek a training in accordance with their own natural desires and abilities."

By 19 December 1945 the remand home was closed and in the middle of the next year there was a new management committee overseeing the rebuilding of the war damaged cottages and school. Shirley re-opened as a children's home in 1947.

After the Second World War

In October 1947, 260 children resided at Shirley. A total of 315 children lived at the Home in July 1948, though there was accommodation for 369 boys and girls.

Boys and girls happily sharing meals together, 1949

A similar establishment, The Hollies in Sidcup, gave the following instructions for arrival of children at the Home: "Let it definitely and clearly be made manifest what the governing aspect symbolises: friendliness, protection, safety, brightness and consideration, and a kindly atmosphere, and if it is a wayward child, it is still a Home for him.

"First impressions are important: the child is suffering from great emotional strain by estrangement from home, parents and old familiar faces and surroundings. It experiences fear. Parents or friends leave him manifesting sorrow and distress.

"They should come in the mornings and a bright room, tastefully decorated, toys and a bowl of goldfish, etc, should be provided in the reception room. Such an atmosphere will impress itself on the child's mind and allay suspicion and fear."

In 1949 the LCC children's committee agreed to rebuild the original twinned cottages of Bramble/Birch, and Chestnut/Daisy which had been "badly damaged" during the war. The new building cost £28,700, which was offset by a grant of £22,520 available from the War Damage Commission. The Committee said the new buildings would be "improved and be of better standard" than the old pairs, particularly in regard to sanitary accommodation and heating. Each cottage would house 20 children and four staff.

Fun in the sun – toddlers at play in a happy nursery environment, June 1949

Nursery

For the first time toddlers attending the nursery at Shirley were integrated with "older age children" cottages. Before summer 1949, nursery-aged children resided in Hawthorn/ Hazel and Holly/Heather Cottages. It was anticipated that nursery-aged children would initially have their midday meal in their

Cheerful girls in a homely atmosphere; and below, an inquisitive nursery group, June 1949

respective cottages. Meals could be provided, if practical, on the nursery premises, for those children who lived in cottages some distance from the nursery.

Even as late as 1949 it was reported: "Unfortunately many children are being admitted in a dirty and verminous condition. One child had crab lice and nits in its eyelids."

In the late 1940s a 'holiday homes' scheme – a type of fostering – was started. In 1949, 50 boys and 30 girls went to 'holiday homes' while 25 boys and 13 girls went to relatives.

After the Second World War the role of industrial training diminished. Soon children in care received no more vocational training than children outside, in keeping with the tendency to make the lives of children in care comparable with those outside, but adding to the difficulty children felt when they left the Home and tried to find work. In the early 1930s the farm had kept 100 poultry and 200 pigs but after the Second World War, when the school re-opened as a junior school and seniors went to a local school nearby, there were no older boys to help with the farm work and the staff could not cope. Pigs and poultry were never again maintained, and the farm fell into disuse.

The 1950s

From the 1950s the character of the Home slowly changed for a number of reasons: general social change with the disappearance of an agreed set of social values; a decline in morale of staff; and the increasing number of children sent to the Home from the courts.

When children reached secondary school age they were sent to schools outside the Home. Since the children were under the care and authority of the LCC, they had to go to schools in London. So children were sent to the nearest LCC schools to the Home. This created problems. The children from the Home did not get on with the local children, and there were constant feuds. Additionally, another school would organise lunch-time raids on the school used by the Shirley children.

A decision was taken in principle as early as 1950 to close the Home, but this was not implemented by the London County Council. For the first time too, some children were allowed home to return to their parents for weekend visits and longer trial periods. In 1950 the LCC children's committee brought recreation ground equipment from Croydon Council. This included a slide, a set of swings climbing frame and a roundabout.

A Home Office circular of 1951 recommended children of all ages to be living in the same cottage, with at least one baby, with a house father who would go out to work and a house mother who would stay at the home, in an idealised picture of what family life should be. It does not seem to have happened at Shirley and was impractical, but is an interesting pointer towards the direction

child care was taking: away from institutions and towards fostering. In the early 1950s, another change took place. Until this time the Headmaster of the Home also held the dual post of Headmaster of the primary school. County Hall decided that the primary school should be administered by the Education Committee and the Home by the Children's Department. The existing Head was given the option of either being Headmaster or Superintendent. He decided to resign. Mr Knight (already Senior Assistant Teacher) was appointed Headmaster and the school was re-named Shirley County Primary School. Mr Mott joined the staff of the school to fill the vacancy left by Mr Knight's promotion.

Mr Heap was appointed Superintendent, instructed by the LCC to prepare the children and staff at Shirley for the eventual closure of the Home. He inherited an ageing staff.

Also in the 1950s the segregation of boys and girls in the cottages was completely

A sunny playgroup in the grassed area of a cottage background, June 1949

discontinued. The old toilets at the end of the school playground were demolished, with the barrier fence removed. Many other changes were in the pipeline. Re-building work now started on part of the school that was bombed during the Second World War. Nearly half the school building was put out of action. New indoor toilets plus cloakrooms were built, with the two derelict classrooms repaired and put into use again. A smart new handicraft room and studio were added, complete with a kiln. The cottages had an extension built at the back and two bathrooms installed. The toilets and basins in the outhouses fell into disuse.

In December 1952 corporal punishment could be administered only with the hand or with a cane of approved pattern. Two canes were approved, a large for boys over 11 and a small one for younger boys and all girls. Girls had to be punished by a woman.

In 1952 a league table was made up of the numbers of children in various establishments spending holidays away from the Home with parents (47) or with 'uncles and aunts' (89). In 1955, 'uncles and aunts' were paid £4 4s a week to take children away on holiday.

For Open Day 1953 a report noted: "The children were able – and anxious – to invite their 'aunties' and their families here to tea, and were able to show them round the homes. From the children's point of view, this was a great event, and they played hosts and hostesses with much enthusiasm."

'Uncles' were given less prominence in time, and in March 1954 128 'aunties' were recruited through the *Sunday Pictorial's* Christmas Appeal. There were problems with some applicants, many lived too far away, "or only wished to befriend the child whose name the Pictorial gave them". The managing committee at Shirley does not appear to have had any suspicions of the motives of people who volunteered to be 'aunties' and 'uncles'.

The new Superintendent of the Home wanted to change the situation with the secondary children going to the two LCC schools. He approached the Croydon Education Department and, with the approval of the headteachers, arrangements were made for a number of children to attend schools in the area. Soon, children would attend Ashburton Secondary, Davidson, Tavistock and the newly-built Shirley High School.

Mr Heap and Miss Pinner adopted a visionary and innovative style to their responsibilities. They had a hands-on approach when working with houseparents, providing valued support, such as visiting cottages regularly and listening carefully to their staff, as well as encouraging them to talk about their role as houseparents. In-house training was given to some staff, though the difficulty remained regulating and monitoring what was happening in some of the cottages.

The staff were invited to choose a new name for the Home by way of a competition. The name was changed from Shirley Residential School to Shirley Oaks in 1955.

These changes served to create a new liberal atmosphere in the Home. The iron gates that guarded the entrance to the Home and stopped children from running away were taken down. This further showed a more positive approach of openness to the outside world. Some housemothers encouraged children to invite their school friends home to tea and to accept invitations to return. Fresh attempts were made to recruit local aunts and uncles, people in the neighbourhood of the Home who were willing to take an interest in an otherwise friendless child. This scheme was successful and in some cases aunts and uncles became foster-parents and eventually adopted a child.

The Home's food and clothes stores were converted into shops. Older children were encouraged to accompany their house-mothers to buy clothes and groceries at the Home shops or in Croydon so that children would get a better idea of housekeeping.

Housemothers were given greater freedom to plan their own meals. The matron's role became less obtrusive in ensuring the smooth running of cottages.

The LCC applied for planning permission to build two semi-detached houses. Their request was granted and Cedar/Romun and Whitehorn/Hawthorn were occupied by the middle of the 1960s. The former was built opposite Beech Cottage, with the latter positioned towards the north east boundary of the Home, close to the laundry and shoe-menders. These houses were to accommodate 12 children.

Recreation

In April 1950 pocket money was set at 1d for children of 3–4, 6d for children of 11 and 12, and five shillings for 17 year olds.

On 1 June 1951 school closed for a Festival of Britain holiday and children went to see Cinderella at West Wickham Theatre.

Nine children went to the procession for the coronation of Queen Elizabeth II in June 1952. Those back in Shirley attended coronation parties. All children were given mugs and coronation chocolate medallions. Twelve children were invited by a Shirley resident to view the coronation on television. Later, 218 children and staff went to London to see the illuminations. Numerous local organisations invited children from Shirley to their Christmas parties.

Staff

In 1954 the Headmaster, A. W. Instrell, received £805 a year plus board, lodging, laundry and so on, valued at £270 a year.

Summer 1955 was the last time the Shirley children went to the LCC Martello Camp at Walton-on-the-Naze, along with those from other large homes, making a group of 7-8,000 children. The Superintendent later wrote: "The Shirley staff consisted of four men and about 70 ladies, not many of them at all keen

on camping, particularly when it rained and the tents leaked! The noise in the huge dining hall supplied with enamel mugs and plates being used by hundreds of excited and happy children, was deafening.

The daily swim in the sea, arranged for the whole camp for safety reasons, although a little noisy, was another major event. The staff who could swim set the perimeter of the bathing area, and children were not allowed to enter the water until the Superintendent blew the whistle. This may sound an easy situation to control, but the beach at Walton is fairly narrow, and in August it had to be shared with all the normal holiday visitors and their children. However, there was to be no doubt about who was staying at the Martello Camp, for when zero hour approached, the beach was invaded by hundreds of youngsters with towels with the words LONDON COUNTY COUNCIL woven in red in big, bold letters down the middle."

There was always some doubt if this colourful invasion was appreciated by the other holiday-makers, but they did have the pleasure of the Shirley band playing hymns on the esplanade each Sunday.

From 1956 onwards, the cottage holidays were very different. Several went abroad, tents were out of favour, at least for cottage holidays, but were used for outward-bound activities.

The 1960s

Organised leisure activities in 1960 included swimming and life-saving, brass band, physical training (games and agility club), art, recorders, pottery, basketry, rug-making, hockey, cricket, football, indoor football, dancing (ballroom and ballet), badminton and tennis. There was a reading club for backward readers, an 'outward bound' club, and a weekly film show in winter. Throughout the 1960s, most cottages still subscribed to the weekly educational magazine *Look and Learn*.

In the early 1960s a community centre was

built. This prefabricated building was erected to free the school's wooden block floors from over exposure. The hall was used for such activities as children's ballet and dance classes. Under the tutorship of Miss M. L. Mead, shows were presented with children dressed in a variety of impressive costumes designed and often made by Miss Mead. On two evenings a week games were organised by a play scheme leader. These games and activities were divided into one hour sessions, for children of all ages.

During the autumn and winter the school hall was used for games and five-a-side football. Lots of enjoyment and fun was experienced, especially when, as on many occasions, five boys played against eight girls. Each team had its own colour or number marked on a wooden block. When a team lost a match, their square block was dropped into a tube. When it reached the bottom it was once again their turn to resume playing.

As was to be expected, particularly during the summer, the Home's swimming pool proved very popular. On Monday mornings the pool's heating was switched on. The water was usually extremely cold, gradually becoming a little warmer as each day passed. On Saturday, the heating was turned off, yet this neither dampened the enthusiasm nor discouraged children from going swimming.

Along each side of the pool there were then about 20 white metal cubicles. Children sometimes shared one between two or even three, depending on the demand. On one occasion, a little girl dropped a glass bottle in her eagerness to get into the pool. The glass shattered everywhere, falling into the water. Swimming had to be stopped until the glass was cleared. Swimming was so popular at the Home that in the summer months the pool would not be hired out to organisations and schools outside the establishment.

Children from Shirley competed against Beecholme Children's Home. This would take

the form of sports events in the morning and a swimming gala held during the afternoon. Shirley produced some very competitive swimmers, some of whom represented Croydon and Surrey.

The summer brought a different interpretation of football from the conventional kind. Boys and girls were divided into two teams each consisting of 20 children or more. The two sets of goal posts were positioned at least a quarter of eat fun was had running and kicking the ball over fields, ditches and past trees to try and score a goal. Understandably, everyone slept well at night.

One game played during the summer holidays consisted of children split into four groups, each controlled by at least one student (students helped in the summer). The object of the exercise was for each team to stay together and make their own way back to Shirley Oaks from Farleigh Common, near Chelsham, Surrey. The children and the students were driven to Farleigh the long way round, to add confusion. The winning team would be the first team that arrived back at Shirley Oaks and managed to locate Mr Len Chatterton, challenging him for the note inside his shoe. This may seem crazy, but the children had great fun.

Another activity that was encouraged was a nature trail. Small groups of four or five children went around the grounds collecting as many insects and animals as they could find within a given time. Some children had match boxes containing spiders, ants, worms and flies of every kind. One child even brought the cottage dog and cat!

Housemothers were encouraged by children to watch the annual Christmas Show held at the school. A group of children, each carrying a placard, would visit the cottages. When the housemother answered the bell and opened the front door, she would be greeted with large words on the placards that a child would be holding, inviting them and telling the time and date. The housemothers were treated to the talents of the children, who entertained them by singing songs, telling jokes and performing skills they felt confident about in the presence of their peers and housemothers.

On a snowy winter's day boys from Shirley Oaks entered a cross country race at Epsom Downs, near the race-course. This event was organised by the Surrey Boys Club. En route to Epsom, the school bus paused at some traffic lights close to a bus stop, whereupon one small boy wound down his window and squirted his bottle over people in the queue. The driver, who had no helpers on that occasion, moved off as quickly as possible, leaving behind disgruntled people shaking their fists at the boys. Needless to say it was only after the event that the driver could see the funny side of what happened. The boys competed very well in the race, displaying great determination.

Blue Peter Club

In 1959 the superintendent of Shirley Oaks met John Nelson, retired policeman, who ran an Outward-Bound section at Sir Philip Games' Boys Club in Addiscombe. The Club was founded and run by police. Local businesses and industries sent their apprentices to Outward Bound Schools on four weeks courses of intensive survival trainingfor team and character building. The Outward Bound Associations throughout the country raised money to send young people otheryoung people on the courses to provide a follow-up in their area when they returned.

About the same time, the Duke of Edinburgh was trying out his idea to give young people the opportunity of achieving an Award, and in so doing, obtain skills and self esteem. It was felt that those in the Outward Bound Group doing the Award could do their

Service to the Community Section by running a Boys' Club in Shirley Oaks. It was also the aim to get all the boys to do the Duke of Edinburgh's Awards themselves. Mr Heap, the superintendent, placed great value on the work and Tony Harris, one of the OB volunteers soon became a full time assistant housefather with the responsibility to develop the Club and the Award.

Membership of the Club was restricted to the boys who were 14 years and over. Some housemothers were glad to get rid of them for the evenings and weekends, provided they had done their chores (and the boys were glad to get away from the cottages, the housemothers and the chores!).

A competition was held to find a name for the Club. The winning title was 'The Blue Peter Club'. The club badge had two signal flags like those used in the navy to signal that a ship was 'outward bound'. This was long before the BBC programme of the same name.

The Club's avowed aim was: "To help and educate boys through their leisure time activities, so as to develop their physical, mental and spiritual capacities that they grow to full maturity as individuals and members of society." The Club was affiliated to the Surrey

The aerial runway assault course activity

The old Shirley Oaks Dormobile used by Club members for expeditions

Blue Peter Club activities at Box Hill, 1961

Club members camping at Box Hill, 1961

Association of Boys' Clubs, which gave it automatic affiliation to the National Association of Boys' Clubs and the sports competitions and outdoor events they held. This gave them opportunities to pursue some sections of the Award.

The Award was divided into four sections. *Service to the Community* – all the members received training from the St. John's Ambulance Brigade and had to pass the basic first aid test.

Pursuits – boys had to choose and pursue a hobby for six months demonstrating their ability to persevere and achieve given standards. The boys found this the most difficult section to complete, despite the large number of options available, sustaining interest and reaching the standard was hard for them.

Expeditions – to achieve this boys received training in the Country Code, camping, cooking, map and compass reading. The old apple shed was cleaned out and decorated by the OB volunteers and Shirley Oaks boys where they met several evenings a week. The Club soon began to acquire its own camping equipment, personal equipment (anoraks, boots), and other apparatus for rock climbing. A room in the farm building was allocated as a store. They received their training in tent pitching and camp cooking in the orchard and then went to the OB campsite at Upper Gatton Park, Merstham, where they learnt to tie knots, splice ropes and construct a rope course. Later a rope and assault course was created with a three high rope bridge from the oak tree behind the Shirley Oaks administrative block to the poplar trees, with an aerial runway down to the apple shed. Due to the interest of several of the voluntary leaders in rock-climbing, camping and climbing used to take place at High Rocks (Tunbridge Wells, Kent) with additional help from the Sandstone Climbing Club. Other 'expeditions' regularly took place to Snowdonia and the Lake District with one to

Dartmoor. These all provided serious training in mountaineering which culminated in August 1963 when the Blue Peter Club joined with Sedgehill Comprehensive School, Bromley, to mount an expedition to the Swiss Alps. The school travelled by train whilst the club went in the old Shirley Oaks Dormobile. Camping 9,000 ft up in the Alps at Arolla they successfully climbed 14,000ft Mont Blanc de Chillon.

Fitness – boys had to achieve a given target in a number of skills including running, jumping, throwing, football dribbling, and so on. Most of the boys were fit and had no difficulty passing this section. In September 1962 the Club was honoured by a visit from Sir John Hunt, the Leader of the successful 1953 Mount Everest Expedition and Director of the Duke of Edinburgh Award Scheme. He spent the day watching demonstrations by the boys of all the skills they had learned before presenting them with the Bronze Awards they had earned. The boy who had abseiled numerous times without any trouble froze when demonstrating it to Sir John Hunt out of

Preparing for sports day, 1960s

one of the Shirley Oaks trees. The other entertainment was Sir John going round the orienteering course at Gatton following the boys and coming back, like them, covered in blackberry stains!

Almond House

Almond House in Wickham Road, Shirley, was a girls' after-care hostel, taking Shirley girls of 15 and over. In December 1956 the warden wrote in a report: "The general conduct of the girls is very poor, the majority are completely irresponsible, take days off from their employment as they like, use very bad language, and are abusive to staff. It is appreciated that the girls have had so many changes of staff and accommodation, that it has been difficult to build and maintain any form of loyalty or respect."

The warden attempted to persuade them "to make more active use of their leisure time, with Sunday afternoon walks, Wednesday evening swimming, and Saturday attendance at football matches...It is hoped that eventually we may be able to further extend our activities to try and counter-balance the hours spent watching TV or playing rock 'n' roll records."

The distinction was made between 'difficult' girls, and 'normal' girls. For example, in a report of 2 November 1956, there is concern for "the hardship which falls on normal girls, in the committee's care, who have to be maintained in hostels, during the periods when difficult girls are also accommodated who often proceed to make life a burden for the officers and the normal girls".

There were great fears that the 'difficult' girls would encourage the 'normal' girls to be more wayward. Part of the answer was a committee of girls who ran much of the hostel and attempted to encourage self-discipline. A note from the Girls' Committee given to all new entrants, headed 'How to make the best of your stay here!', introduced ideas like a rota for housework and advised "our experience is that we need to stay indoors in the hostel about two nights every week to give us time for washing and mending our clothes and generally looking after personal requirements ... Boyfriends who have been introduced to the warden are allowed to visit at times to be settled by her."

To humanise the establishment, girls brought flowers in and purchased their own bath towels, withdrawing the ones with LCC stamped on them. They went on to replace LCC tea towels, crockery and the like with ordinary ware. The warden reported in July 1957: "As these girls will be the wives and mothers of the future, it is felt that housekeeping – especially the basic financial rudiments of running a home – should be an essential part of their training.

Staff

There had been a gradual change in management structure, handing over the authority of the Superintendent in day-to-day tasks to the houseparents. They took over the ordering of provisions, payment of pocket money, purchase of clothing and the arrangement of children's annual holidays. They were required to keep within an agreed budget figure based on the number and ages of the children in each house. There were initial difficulties with self-budgeting but eventually the exercise in autonomy of individual homes was successful. The existing clothing store was fitted out as a shop, although older children could be taken out to local shops.

The staff had problems of their own. On 6 June 1955 the suicide of a housemother was reported – the unfortunate woman was found dead by one of the children in her gas-filled kitchen. Staff showed great loyalty to the Home and some children stayed on as staff. There were real staff difficulties, however, with the necessity of staff cover for the homes 24

hours a day. The problem was one of giving the children an adequate standard of care while also permitting staff reasonable hours of work. After many staff meetings in the 1950s and 60s a workable solution was reached: in each house a small staff team of two people was established. They were resident and were prepared to make up for the long hours by having definite time off each day, long weekends periodically and having extra days added to annual leave. This team was supplemented by a regular, non-resident daily domestic. In 1961 there were 401 children at the Home, with 90 staff.

Staff had differing ideas on their role. Some wanted to be 'parents' to their residents. They could be strict disciplinarian types or protective 'molly-coddlers'. Other staff acted as 'power to young people' advocates who said the residents should define their own boundaries and should have freedom of expression.

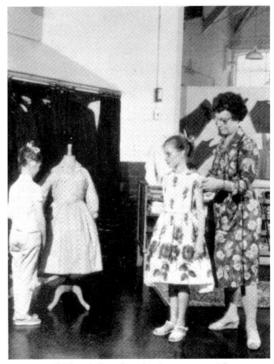

Shirley clothes shop for the younger girls

It was an unusual upbringing for children in long-term care, but some of them did manage to bond with staff, sharing happy, sad and bewildering times.

Intake

In the moral atmosphere of the post-war period, much thought was given to the question of giving children a new start. The Children's Officer on 20 May 1950 reported: "Children committed to the care of the council are, in the majority of cases, such as are deemed to be in need of care and protection, not because they themselves have been guilty of any offences, but generally because they are the sufferers from parental neglect or ill treatment. A minority have been delinquent, generally in a minor way, but the courts have usually committed such children to the care of the council because the delinquency has been deemed to be due to or

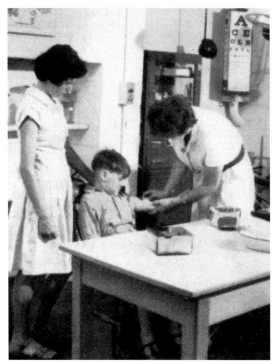

The Shirley infirmary, early 1960s

aggravated by an unsuitable home background. Occasionally a child is committed to the care of the council because he has failed to attend school regularly."

Many were short-stay children. An LCC publication of 1962 called *In London's Care* noted that 12,000 applications were made a year for children to go into care. "The temporary illness or confinement of the mother gives rise to more applications than any other single cause, and about half the children received into care in a recent year came into the Council 'family' for that reason." In Shirley, the turnover in 1958 was 50%. There was a stable population, but also a constant number of short-stay children. Throughout the late 1950s, the number of children at the Home slowly declined. By 1959 there were 370 children, of whom 259 had families.

The Welfare Officer wrote on 8 March 1949: "There is still a great deal to be done in making home visits to gain a clear insight into the family background, so as to assist the children who build up a defence against their feelings and longings, and others who show their suffering in outward behaviour. It is so essential to try and keep the children in contact with their relations. Unfortunately, many of those children in most need of personal affection and reassurance are frequently those who have developed the most difficult behaviour traits and therefore least acceptable. Contact must always be maintained between them through the Child Welfare Officer, with the agreement and co-operation of foster parents". Like many theoretical arrangements which relied on goodwill, this would break down easily, in some cases leaving children not knowing that they even had siblings who had been fostered while they stayed in care.

In a report to prospective child care staff, the Superintendent, Clifford Heap, wrote in 1959: "Most parents are surprised to find that only a few children in care are orphans.

Parents are very much 'in the picture', and an important part of our job is concerned with making a relationship with them and any other interested outsiders. Many of our children go home for days, week-ends, and holidays, and parents are encouraged to visit as frequently as possible, thus, while providing a stable and secure environment for the children, we must not become so possessive as to resent parents' visits. We must never forget that the parents we possibly find difficult and hard to understand, are an essential part of the lives of their children."

There were specific instructions to cover the situation when one child was fostered and another was not, as mentioned in a report of the Children's Officer of 12 March 1954.

When children took their 11-plus, they were sent to different schools. In 1960, pupils of 27 London and Croydon schools lived at Shirley Oaks, while travelling each day to school.

On 12 January 1962 there were 396 children at Shirley: 245 boys and 151 girls. In 1962 all the large cottage bedrooms were partitioned into two rooms so that children could have more privacy. In 1962 a 17-year old still at school would receive 35s a week pocket money, which included a clothing allowance. In 1960 a part-time houseparent earned £9 a week with free board and lodging.

CHAPTER FOUR

The London Borough of Lambeth

In 1965 there was a local government shake-up when the London County Council was disbanded and the Greater London Council took over, with responsibility for the children's homes being handed over to individual boroughs. The London Borough of Lambeth was given Shirley Oaks Children's Home in April 1965 and responsibility for the school was given to the Inner London Education Authority. They considered the cottages 'obsolete' and unsuitable for the present day needs of children in care.

This was an uncertain and unsettling time for staff and housemothers. A number who were approaching retirement chose to do so. Others decided to leave because of the uncertainty about the future.

When the handover to the London boroughs took place, all the operational functions of the Home ceased overnight from 31 March to 1 April.

Any children who came from other London boroughs were transferred, in due course, to homes run by those boroughs. This created many problems in the lives of some children, who were moved when they were happy at Shirley. This was fundamentally against the principles of child care: the interests of the children should come first. The interests of the children were being sacrificed for administrative simplicity. It was an important staging post in the decline in standards of child care in the post-war period.

Shirley suffered an accelerating decline, hastened by the twin policies of fostering as many children as possible and having children's homes as part of the community. This meant, for example, that when a new housing estate was to be built, a children's home would be built with it, or a large family house would be purchased, looking no different from others in the street, and converted into a children's home for a small number of children.

Lambeth made some significant changes to the running of Shirley Oaks. The post of matron gradually disappeared and house-parents were referred to by their first names or as 'uncle' or 'auntie'. Houseparents now had much more power over the children, making decisions about where they should go to secondary school.

Children were given their own money to spend outside the Home, and were sometimes sent out to the shops by houseparents; older children bought their own clothes. Some of these reforms were already in place when Lambeth took over, but the Borough consolidated them. Other changes that affected the weekly running of each cottage concerned the purchasing of household provisions. Receipts had to be kept of all groceries, domestic items and children's clothes. These were listed in a petty cash book with two copies submitted to Lambeth at Blue Star House. Sometimes there would be audits made. This procedure gave even more autonomy to the housemothers, as well as more administration.

The Home's food, clothing and utensils

stores soon closed. Thus the cottages at Shirley obtained a stronger degree of independence. The sewing-room continued functioning for a time at a very reduced level, mostly making children's name tapes and marking linen with cottage names. No alterations to clothes were undertaken; these were handled by cottage staff or the children themselves. Maintenance services and repairs, along with gardening were retained.

Children no longer took their shoes to be re-heeled and re-soled at the Home's shoe shop. Previously, two cobblers had been employed to mend shoes, either while children waited or to be collected later.

The new administration introduced a monthly publication called *The Shirley Oaks magazine*. It gave news on events at the Home, staff changes, features on daily outings, and pictures drawn by the children. In addition to stories and poems written by staff it would give results of competitions like the Miss Shirley Oaks contest. The magazine ran until the late 1960s. Below is a poem and a limerick reproduced from the magazine.

Another Pearl from our Wild Poetess – "A Vain Dream" (written just before the sweep was due to arrive).

> *As I sit in my Cottage from dawn till dust,*
> *there's just one thing which I yearn for and lust*
> *some form of central heating.*
> *How much cleaner, easier too,*
> *and so less work for me (and you).*
> *The metal monster, standing there,*
> *drives me into the depths of despair.*
> *It's never alight when the weather is cold,*
> *and just like the kids, it won't do as it's told.*
> *When I go to bed at night,*
> *there it is all burning bright.*
> *I check no dead coke is there within*
> *the ash and clinkers in the bin.*
> *6.45, I'm up and about*
> *to find the dratted thing's gone out.*
> *Down on my knees midst coke and dust,*
> *dreaming of that for which I lust,*
> *some form of central heating.*
> *What are the chances, I ask you,*
> *of ever seeing my dreams come true?*

> *"Round the Houses Limericks (22)"*
> *The best way to get around 'Sycamore'*
> *Is to charge like a bull-fighting picador.*
> *Then, instead of 'Hooray'*
> *we can all shout 'Ole'*
> *Like a Spaniard just home from Arkansas.*
> (very subtle this!)

When children became ill, they no longer stayed in the Home's infirmary. Instead provision was made either in the cottage or, in more serious cases, treatment was handled by Mayday Hospital or Queen Mary's Children's Hospital at Carshalton. While a surgery still remained on the site, it dealt with prescriptions and residential health issues. The surgery moved to new premises at Aster House, a home previously used for adolescent boys and a former staff sleeping quarters. Willow Cottage was converted into sleeping accommodation for the staff, sometimes being used for their training. The former infirmary was used as a home for mentally and physically disabled children.

In the early 1970s there were less than 250 children residing at the Home and this number declined throughout the decade. A larger than usual number of staff, who had given many years of service, either left or retired. Mrs Boulton, who worked in the laundry for many years, and Miss Bryan, who worked in the nursery, both retired. A presentation was made to each of them.

Over the next two decades, some of the cottages fell into disuse. Often these cottages would be reoccupied by staff and children. From the end of the 1970s a noticeable number of cottages was empty for the remainder of the Home's existence. Staff morale was affected by the behavioural and emotional problems of some children, which some carers found difficult to cope with, not least because they had little support and no training in this area. There were also staff shortages because of the long hours and relatively low pay this testing full time work attracted. The wages for an assistant part-time housemother in 1969 were £17 10s for a 24-hour week. High staff turnover remained a problem.

During the 1970s it was felt by some observers that some of the Home's administrators were setting their own priorities and staff were looking to their own interests. There were tensions when some staff and residents felt that houseparents relaxed the house rules in favour of the children from their own cottage. The chronic staff shortages put pressure on the remaining staff to cover any unfilled vacancies. The management of the Home was keen to obtain residential staff, but even more desperate to retain their services as they were difficult to replace.

Housemothers had different philosophies towards youngsters who came to play from different cottages. They openly discouraged children from other cottages mixing with their own, fearing that the other children would be a bad influence, or disapproving of how other housemothers ran their cottage. This brought into contrast the different styles and methods housemothers had in bringing up children. Some housemothers believed that they and their assistants should do all the work, while others felt children should do chores such as wiping-up plates after meals, fetching coal from the coal bunker to place next to the fireplace, laying tables and putting utensils away after use.

Children who were in long-term care generally treated Shirley as their home, whether they were entirely happy or not. For children who lived there for short stays, the Home may have had less significance in their lives. Inevitably, they would be less settled and were perhaps more likely to be unhappy.

Shirley Oaks Primary School

Towards the late 1960s, the Home's brass band, which had been such a feature in the history of Shirley since its inception, fell into terminal decline. Soon the band's only engagement would be playing on Monday morning at the school assembly.

On Thursday morning, lessons started with religious instruction. These classes were given by the respective chaplains of the Anglican, Methodist and Roman Catholic churches. On Friday afternoons children watched films such as "The Life of Eskimos", "The Production of Coca Beans from Guyana", films about the culture of the Chinese Emoire, Insects and other aspects of the natural world.

At school on 1 July 1969, children watched on television the investiture of Prince Charles as the 21st Prince of Wales at Caernarvon Castle. In the late 1960s open days included fancy dress competitions, 'It's a Knockout' races, and a colourful pageant tracing the history of the Home.

Gymnastics remained very much part of the children's physical sport. Activities included

Sack race at Shirley Sports Day, 1969

forward and backward rolls, cartwheels, hand springs, flip-flaps, vaulting over a horse and handstands, all performed on the green mats, often with more enthusiasm than skill, but occasionally with precision.

After-school activities included the game 'king of the jungle'. All the gym apparatus, climbing frames, ropes, mats and benches were set up so that children could go all around and cross the hall without touching the floor. One of the children had to chase everyone and touch them. Those touched or who touched the floor had to sit on the stage until the last person was king of the jungle. If the person doing the chasing touched the floor everyone on the stage was allowed back on.

Teachers and children of school-leaving age at Shirley Oaks Primary undertook annual residential trips. Ilfracombe and Rhyl in Wales were popular resorts. After leaving the junior school children would attend secondary schools in the area, some Catholic children would attend St Thomas More and later a few went to St Mary's High School.

Christmas

In common with most schools, Shirley Primary performed Christmas plays, with house-parents and staff in attendance. The children from each year group took part in imaginative and creative hat competitions. Food parcels made up from gifts given during the harvest festival were distributed to local elderly people living in Addiscombe.

Annual carol services were held a couple of nights before Christmas. These services took place close to the main entrance to the Homes, close to Almond House, where once a giant evergreen tree stood, suitably trans-formed into a Christmas tree. All the clergy from the parish attended, taking turns in leading the service each year. This event brought together children and staff, as well as people from the local community around a nativity crib.

A custom that originated from the 1960s involved the superintendent, accompanied by Shirley Oaks officials and Father Christmas visiting each cottage to wish children and staff the compliments of the season. Bell-ringing would announce their arrival. Sometimes the sound would bring relief to the faces of the housemothers who, until then, would not know when this company might arrive. The Home's officials would give small gifts to each child. Before leaving to make their next call, the two staff would receive thanks in appreciation for their efforts: a box of chocolates or packet of cigarettes.

The *Daily Express* newspaper and the Variety Club of Great Britain were among organisations that hosted annual Christmas parties for Shirley children. To mark the Queen's Silver Jubilee year in 1977, the Variety Club held a huge summer event in Hyde Park for deprived children from all over London. It was dubbed the world's biggest party, with Shirley children in attendance. They became engrossed in the longest sausage and biggest jelly in the world!

The Variety Club also gave free tickets to the Home for the Royal Tournament, London theatre land, pantomimes and shows at the Fairfield Halls. Children also went on day trips to places like Littlehampton and Brighton.

Recreation

During the 1970s Shirley's tradition for sporting activities continued. Football remained the primary game for most of the boys, while rounders was also popular. Other out-door pursuits included hide and seek, and knock-down ginger. Throughout the year the primary school was the host for many after-school clubs and classes which included art, pottery, needlework, basket-making, and ballroom and tap-dancing. The Community Centre showed a film during the week, as well as holding country dancing lessons on a Friday evening. Summer play schemes were organised to keep youngsters from becoming restless, including swimming, football, talent competitions, cricket, treasure hunts, drawing competitions, trips to Shirley Hills and one-day outings. Before the close of the decade, however, such activities were curtailed.

The school's reputation for swimming continued. Crystal Palace national pool was the venue where these skills were refined.

The Home's 'Open Day' was usually combined with the primary school's open afternoon or evening.

The Shirley Oaks Primary School sports day consisted of a swimming gala and sports afternoon. Houseparents were encouraged to come to the latter and often found themselves entering into the spirit of the event by competing in an egg and spoon race, sack race, wheel-barrow race, or something similar. Each child was assigned to one of four teams

Shirley 'Open Day', 1969

that were named after colours: blue, red, yellow and green.

Crystal Palace Football Club provided complementary tickets for their home games. Children would experience the high and lows of this colour club

Cottages went camping to Henfield in West Sussex for the weekends or even longer stays in the summer. In the early 1970s, school journeys were curtailed in favour of day trips. Shortly after the 1970 Olympic Games, Miss Wilson, who swam for England, was appointed the school swimming teacher.

An adventure playground was built at the entrance of the piggery. A mud mound was constructed, reinforced by a concrete floor, with a breeze block forming a castle wall. A climbing frame with nets, sailing boats set in concrete and a disused mangled jeep were other popular attractions. This venue had always been a meeting place where friendly and not-so-friendly warfare took place. The development of the area, with its bushy features and dense woodland, ensured that children would be able to derive even greater fun from exploration. Informal activities involved children forming small groups and establishing secret hide-outs and camps.

Children wishing to join such groups would have to undergo initiation tests like climbing trees and speed-crawling through underground tunnels competing with water streams.

In response to the hot and humid weather, children were allowed to wear swimming costumes. On such occasions deck chairs would be positioned on the lawns outside the front of some cottages. Afternoon tea, sandwiches, cakes and lemonade were enjoyed by housemothers and children.

The school corresponded with the ship *Varria Cella*, an oil tanker. The crew would write and tell the children about their excursions.

An article in the *Croydon Advertiser* dated 19 July 1970, under the heading: 'Group hand over their contribution to happiness', stated:

A new playground for under sevens which has been paid for by the Croydon and District Auctioneers and Surveyors Assoc-iation, was handed over to Shirley Oaks Children's Home on Sunday.

The Association raised £340 for equipment, and the playground itself was built by the housefathers at Shirley Oaks.

Mr Trevor Burrage, the last year's President of the Association, said at the handing over ceremony: 'It is the house fathers who made sure our money has gone so far. A tremendous amount of effort has gone into it, and if professional labour had been used, it would have cost twice as much'.

Counsellor R Greenwood, Chairman of Lambeth's newly formed Social Services Committee, who has responsibility for Shirley Oaks, replying on behalf of the Borough, said: "Shirley Oaks is very go-ahead organisation, and Lambeth are very grateful that we have got such a good staff".

Also at the ceremony was Ald. G. Hickmore, Lambeth's deputy mayor and chairman of the Children's Committee before the reorganisation.

"You cannot put a value on a gift like this" he said, "because you cannot value the happiness of the children".

Most cottages took full advantage of the abundant raspberry and blackberry bushes within the establishment. Pies and crumbles were prepared, some even frozen, to be enjoyed in the winter months. Apples, pears, plums and rhubarb were also plucked from the orchards, and 'nobblers' that tasted like a cherry plum, were eaten with relish.

The widow of Mr Fred Jones, who worked as a gardener at the Home for 45 years, wrote to Shirley Oaks to record her thanks and appreciation for the bouquet of flowers sent for his funeral.

Local companies, such as Marks & Spencer, supported the Home with food. After school, the community centre was used by Marks & Spencer as a base for girls and boys to try out the store's footwear. The children's time and patience would be rewarded with packets of sweets like chocolate eclairs, murray mints, jelly babies and toffees.

Marks & Spencer also provided children with jumpers, shirts, trousers, socks and underwear. Houseparents and their assistants had to record the wash and wear ability of these try-outs over time. Naturally, children had the benefit of keeping these clothes after testing had been completed.

Shirley drew the majority of domestic staff from the surrounding areas, particularly Shirley, New Addington and Shrublands. They worked from about 9am until 1pm. A number of these women took the opportunity to become assistant housemothers.

In the spring of 1973, 23 cottages were in operation. Greater authonomy was given to the houseparents and 194 children lived in the Home. If houseparents were not satisafied with GLC supplies they could now make their own arrangements with purchasing food. Bread, fruit and vegetables were already being brought locally by individual houseparents and this policy was continued.

By 1974 the role of superintendent ceased to exist. Instead there was a non-residential Children's Home Officer, who had responsibility for the overall running of the Home. Answerable to him were a small group of people known as group management officers, who each had half a dozen cottages to administer.

Around the middle of the 1970s, the old solid fuel stoves in the cottage kitchens were replaced with gas boilers, from which came hot water and heating for the homes. Some twinned cottages were re-named to form one residence. Elm/Fern, for example, became known as Elm.

Autonomy

Lambeth's Social Services Department decided on 14 July 1972 that the Home at Shirley Oaks should have greater autonomy.

This would give houseparents greater freedom and more direct responsibility for the running of individual cottages. The trend had turned away from big homes in which all supplies were bought collectively and all decisions made by the superintendent. As a report to Lambeth's Social Services directorate commented: "The object was to give the children a more natural upbringing, to fit them better for the outside world by giving them experience of normal things, such as buying some of their clothing in an ordinary shop with the guidance of their housemothers, so as to avoid the painful emergence into the wide world of a child of fifteen plus, as often happened, completely institutionalised and quite unfitted to look after himself and deal with money."

The council wanted to replace Shirley Oaks as one big school, with a number of smaller homes in keeping with modern child care concepts. An obvious first step was to give houseparents charge of individual cottages. This could easily be done with 13 of the cottages; another five were closed, and another five were devoted to children with special needs, where autonomy would not be possible.

Lambeth Social Services Committee agreed in October 1972 an amended scale of weekly pocket money for children in their residential homes. A baby aged one year would receive 8p a week. This allowance increased by 1p annually until the child reached five years old. Children aged six and ten were paid 14p and 25p respectively. Pocket money went up 20p every year until the child was aged 14. A 17 year old received £2 per week.

Houseparents had to be trained for their new responsibilities. There was discussion about the amount of space they required to carry out their new responsibilities, such as keeping their own files and seeing parents and social workers. The houseparents were concerned that there should be no more than six children per cottage, or eight as an absolute maximum.

Shirley Oaks therefore proceeded with moves towards 'autonomy', but one of the official reports sounded a warning note for the establishment as a whole. "One cannot truly consider the position at Shirley Oaks without realising that it is completely outmoded in its standards. Even with reduced numbers of children, the facilities and accommodation would be totally unacceptable outside the context of this particular type and age of establishment."

New Homes for Lambeth

The Schools made front page news in the *Croydon Advertiser* dated 9 July 1976, under the heading: 'Lambeth win battle of Shirley Oaks'.

"The Go-Ahead has been given for a massive council estate at Shirley Oaks – so bringing a six year battle to a bitter end for Croydon Council.

Mr Peter Shore, Secretary of State for the Environment, has decided that Lambeth Council should be allowed to build homes for 1,500 people on their own land at Shirley Oaks. His decision follows a second public enquiry into the controversial site held in February this year. He says the development must have two access roads leading to Wickham Road and Shirley Road.

Lambeth's scheme for the site was rejected by the Department of the Environment in 1972 because it had only one access road. But the introduction of the second road caused anger among Shirley residents. They thought their homes would become 'sandwiched' between roads, and were also against the development because of the extra traffic it would bring to the area.

Croydon Council wanted development of this site delayed until results of the GLC road development scheme in Shirley and Wickham Road had been assessed. And it was this delay that made Lambeth take Croydon to the second public inquiry on Shirley Oaks.

Lambeth plans for the site – once earmarked for a new Croydon General Hospital – included 472 homes arranged in clusters, and a recreation centre on 25 of the 72 acres. Plans for 11 children's homes have been dropped. The main reason for the DoE giving Lambeth approval for its estate is the Borough's pressing need for homes. But, to safeguard the present interests of Shirley residents, the DoE has made several stipulations about the development.

They are that:

• Homes are to be no more than three stories high. 43 acres of open park and are to be retained around the estate.

• Landscaping should be done before building starts.

• Car parking spaces should be provided.

• A 6ft high fence should be put up along the boundary of houses in Shirley Avenue.

• The Recreation Centre should be sound-proofed, and its use limited to 9.30am to 10pm on Sundays.

• The proposed new access road from Shirley Road

must be completed before any houses are occupied.

• A 6–7ft high bank must be built between the estate and houses fronting the north side of Shirley Avenue.

Mr Martin Stritch, Croydon's Head of Development Planning, said this bank would help eliminate noise from the estate. He added: "It won't improve the view, but it's one of those things that can't be helped". Mr Stritch said he hoped the DoE would approve Lambeth's plans for an estate with only one access road. But he was glad to see the "saga of Shirley Oaks" at an end.

Leading Tories have dismissed suggestions that 1,500 people coming from Labour-controlled Lambeth to Shirley Oaks Council Estate will cause great surprise at future elections.

Croydon North East MP, Mr Bernard Weatherall – who had a majority of 3,000 at the last poll, said: 'It's not true to say all people on council estates vote Labour'.

Shirley Oaks Primary School in the early 1970s, where the present Shirley Oaks Hospital stands

The next weekend the paper reported: "Start on new estate planned for 1979".

It will be about 3 years before Lambeth Council start building their first house at Shirley Oaks.

Lambeth have been given the go-ahead for a massive 472-home estate by Secretary of State for the Environment, Mr Peter Shore. His announcement ended the six year tussle over Shirley Oaks between Croydon, who once wanted to have a new general hospital there, and Lambeth, who own the 72 acres of land.

A major reason for his approval of the project was Lambeth's 'pressing' need for homes. A Lambeth Council spokesman said final detailed plans were yet to be drawn up for Croydon Council's approval. He anticipated that these plans will come to Croydon in 18 to 24 months. If they agreed, building should start in two and a half to three years. Another reason why work could not begin sooner at Shirley Oaks was that it was only a part of Lambeth's extensive programme of home building."

Farewell to the Head

Another event covered by the *Croydon Advertiser*, on 31 July 1970, was the retirement of the Headmaster, under the title: "Head's farewell ends 21 years at school". It read: "Colleagues, education officers and old pupils went to Shirley Oaks Children's Home on Thursday of last week to pay tribute to Mr PT Knight (60) who is retiring as Headmaster of the primary school at the Home...He moved to Shirley Oaks in 1949 as Senior Assistant when the headship of the Home and the school was a combined post. He became Head of the school in 1954.

"Speakers who gathered at the Home's Community Centre included Dr M. C. Roe, an Inner London Education Authority Schools' Inspector, who has special responsibility for special schools, including Shirley Oaks Primary School, who paid tribute. "I honour you for three reasons – for being a very good teacher, and doing remarkably well in

everything you do; for being a good headmaster; and for working so well with people", she told Mr Knight.

"Mr Knight was presented with a cheque...a scroll of the names of people who had contributed, letters of commendation from past pupils and staff, and a car radio. Children contributed to Mr Knight's retirement cheque with each cottage donating at least £1".

Mr Knight's successor altered the school's dinner time. The school stopped for children to go back to their cottages for lunch at noon, instead of 12.25pm. Children would return to school for 1.30pm. School ended at the earlier time of 3.30pm instead of 4p.m. Some housemothers found these changes slightly annoying, because they had less time to settle down the children, when they eventually came back for their dinner. This was especially true when some of the cottages were further from the school than others. At school assemblies, children were reminded to make their way back to their cottage as soon as possible.

By the end of summer 1972, Mr Arthur Mott, who had been at Shirley since 1955, retired as Deputy Head of the school. In 1974 Lambeth Council wrote to the Chaplains stating that they had no formal role at the Home, although they were welcome to visit at the request of individual cottages. In October 1976 the number of children at the Home was 197. There were vacancies for a further 34, and five children were home on trial.

In Autumn 1978 two unions – the National Association for Local Officers and the National Union of Public Employers – asked residential staff to consider strike action in a dispute over pay and conditions. The threat of industrial action was averted but it once again brought into perspective the differing attitudes of full-time staff members. Some houseparents believed striking was not appropriate in residential child care; others understandably sought to improve their employment conditions and salary.

The 1980s

In the early 1980s there were staff training sessions on health and safety and race awareness courses. Staff were strongly encouraged to participate in these seminars.

After a decade of declining numbers of children at the Homes and new approaches to residential child care, plans were made to close Shirley as a children's home. As part of these plans Shirley Oaks Primary School officially closed at the end of the summer term in 1982.

On 5 November 1982 a fire that destroyed Shirley Oaks Primary School made the front page of the Croydon Advertiser, under the heading "Disused school gutted".

About 100 firemen from Croydon and the surrounding areas fought for hours on Wednesday night to quell a blaze which gutted a disused school in Glenthorne Drive, Shirley.

According to firemen, the fire at Shirley Oaks Primary School was the biggest in the area for years. The school was owned by Lambeth Council, and used until recently for pupils from their children's Home at Shirley Oaks. Police at South Norwood and the Fire Brigade are investigating the fire, which is said to be of a suspicious nature.

Police said yesterday (Thursday) that smoke was noticed coming from the school by Mr Arthur Buck of Shirley, who was walking in the area. He called the Brigade after seeing books and papers stacked up in the main classroom.

A divisional fire officer described the fire as 'of doubtful origin' and the fire investigation unit have said it may have been started deliberately by children. The fire began just after 5.30pm and was not finally extinguished until half a hour after midnight, said a spokesman for the Fire Brigade at Woodside. At one time the Brigade had 12 fire engines, a hydraulic tower and two hose lorries on the scene. There were no casualties in the fire".

The report was accompanied by a photograph with the caption: "Flames light up the night sky as the blaze takes hold at the disused Shirley Oaks Primary School". This story made front page news. On 30

Aftermath of the fire which destroyed the School, 5 November 1982

September the *Croydon Advertiser* reported under the heading: "Work to start on 'first' private hospital".

Work on what now seems likely to become Croydon's first private hospital is due to start early next year, it was announced this week.

The 50-bed hospital on the old Shirley Primary School site in Glenthorne Avenue, Shirley, should be finalised by the end of the year. It will cost £3 million to build, and another £700,000 to equip, says the company behind the project, London based Hospital Capital Corporation.

Patients in each of the private 50 private rooms, complete with en suite bathroom, television and telephone, will pay – at today's prices – around £107 a day (the maximum permitted by the main private health insurance schemes). Doctors' fees are extra. Full planning permission for the hospital has just been approved by the Croydon Council...

The new Shirley Oaks Village

The Children's Home was run down and finally closed in 1983, when it was sold as building land to a property development company which converted a few of the cottages but demolished the majority, landscaping the site, and building a vast housing development on it. It is a testimony to the quality of the buildings that, so many years after their establishment, they could be converted and sold to householders as private homes. Opinions differed as to the merits of the redevelopment of the site but Heron Homes earned a National House Building Council award in 1988. Shirley Oaks was judged to be one of the best supervised developments in the Greater London Region.

It was a dignified ending for an institution which had achieved so much.

ON AN 80 ACRE SITE ADJACENT TO THIS PLAQUE STOOD

SHIRLEY OAKS

A HOME FOR CHILDREN IN NEED OF CARE. ORIGINALLY NAMED SHIRLEY RESIDENTIAL SCHOOL, IT WAS BUILT BY THE BERMONDSEY BOARD OF GUARDIANS AND OPENED IN 1903. AT THAT TIME IT WAS A FORWARD LOOKING PROJECT WITH 38 COTTAGES, SICK BAY, SWIMMING BATH, LAUNDRY, WORKSHOPS AND FULL AGE RANGE SCHOOL.

IN 1930 IT WAS TAKEN OVER BY THE LONDON COUNTY COUNCIL WITH WHICH AUTHORITY IT REMAINED UNTIL 1965 WHEN IT WAS TRANSFERRED TO THE LONDON BOROUGH OF LAMBETH.

SHIRLEY OAKS WAS FINALLY CLOSED IN 1983.

SINCE 1903 THOUSANDS OF CHILDREN LIVED HERE, SOME FOR A FEW WEEKS, OTHERS FOR UP TO 15 YEARS. UNTIL THE LATTER YEARS THE DAILY NUMBER ON ROLL RARELY FELL BELOW 400.

THIS PLAQUE MARKS THE PLACE OF SHIRLEY OAKS IN OUR SOCIAL HISTORY AND WAS ERECTED BY A GROUP OF ONE TIME CHILDREN STAFF AND FRIENDS, WHO LIKE THOSE BEFORE THEM SHARED THE MANY HAPPY AND SOMETIMES SAD TIMES THROUGHOUT THE 80 YEARS IT REMAINED OPEN.

Accounts of Life at Shirley

Grace Adams, nee Whitten (1913–1927)

In 1911 my father died in Guys Hospital. He left my mother with seven children: four boys and three girls. There was no child allowance in those days, no income support or housing benefit. So we ended up in the Parish Street Workhouse at Bermondsey overnight.

The next day my brother William and two sisters, Gladys and Esther, were transferred to the Shirley Schools. I did not go and had to stay in Peckham for two years because there were no facilities for babies at Shirley Schools.

My first recollection of Shirley Schools was of a small boy taking off his boots to change into slippers which was something the children had to do before entering the cottage. The small boys up to the age of seven were with the girls over the girls' side of the Home. When they were seven they joined the boys on the boys' side. I was in a single cottage named "Beech". I was sitting on the hearth rug. I had a bald head caused by ringworm caught at Peckham.

Arthur, as I afterwards knew him to be, laughed and laughed. When the housemother asked what he was laughing at he said "she got no hair". "Oh yes", said the housemother, "she has lovely curls, but they are underneath." Arthur and I became friends. He was my boyfriend until he was ten years old and then his uncle came over from America and took him back to America with him. I was devastated and cried for a week.

There used to be a girl called Gladys and she had the same problems. Her hair would not grow so they gave her a Mary Pickford wig with a brush and comb and another wig to wear when one went to the cleaners. I hoped that would happen to me but when they had almost made up their minds my hair started coming through very thin and straggly and they used to call me "nine hairs and a bit of cotton". My sister Esther, had a lovely head of hair with two long plaits down to her waist. On high days and holidays we used to do our hair up in vinegar rags to make it curl. Esther had long ringlets and I had 'cracker nobs' which turned out all frizzy. The housemothers used to ask me "did they hurt?" but I said "no" and then they would say "Pride feels on pain".

There was a little donkey who loved the children and used to bray loudly and frighten the life out of us. There were two shire horses – one named Prince and one named Major. They used to collect the cottages' laundry and take it back again when it was washed. It was a great treat to get a ride on the cart to deliver the clean laundry.

The horses used to pull the mower to cut the grass. Children were not allowed on the grass when it was growing because it was needed for hay. We used to listen to the mower and the noise it made. It was a lovely sound and the smell of newly-cut grass was lovely. I can smell it yet. As soon as it was dry we were allowed to toss it. It was fun.

There were lots of oak trees on the estate and during the 1914 War we could not get enough food for the pigs so we used to collect acorns and take them to the farm and the farmer used to give us four cooking apples for a bucket. Our pigs were famous and they came from everywhere for them. Acorns are not the best diet for pigs but 'any port in a storm'. They had a good pedigree and lived in tiled sties. We had a dog named Gyp and he was on a chain right across the entrance to the farm. If you had to take a message to the farm, Gyp would not let you in.

During the First World War the little ones used to have a bed made up on the pot board in the kitchen. When there were Zeppelin air raids over Shirley, the older children used to stand in the cottage hallway and put the coats that were hanging there over their heads. We were not allowed to talk or scream when the bangs came too near. A Zeppelin came down in flames and you could see it for miles. An enemy air craft came down in Farmer Still's field, They were novelties in those days and everyone came to see them.

My brother was a member of the brass band and played a euphonium. One year they came ninth in the All England Band Contest. We had a choir with about 200 voices. You had to have a medical certificate not to sing in the choir. We used to go down to the assembly hall in the evenings for practice. There were no lights on the road and I was terrified of the dark. The choir got quite famous. When we did plays the choir used to sing Baker Rolle and the Wedding March.

At Christmas we did not have any presents unless our relatives brought them on visiting days. The under-eights used to have a party with Christmas tree and fairy doll on top. How I envied that fairy doll. The older children had entertainments in the Assembly Hall but I was so terrified I didn't enjoy the entertain-ment one bit. The Guardians gave us two apples and oranges each, a tin of biscuits and a bottle of ginger beer. Breakfast on Christmas day was the only time in the year we had a boiled egg.

There were no tarmac roads in those days, just grit and very dirty. We were not allowed to

walk on the path when the Matron and Headmaster were walking on it. We had to go out into the road, which was very dusty. It was a long way between the two gates, one in Wickham Road and the other in Glenthorne Avenue. This was the entrance the teachers used. My brother William was in charge of the gate and he used to have to take the keys down to the lodge gate at Wickham Road every day. He was a nice-looking boy and the Head-master chose him as his Office Boy. He had to go into Croydon on the pony and trap with the Headmaster to take care of the pony while the Headmaster took the Books in for Audit. He left the pony and went off to buy some sweets and the Headmaster came back and found the pony on his own. William was punished severely and sent to work on the farm among the pig sties. It was no punishment to him because he got on well with the farmer, who thought the world of him.

I hated church because we were not allowed to sit in the middle aisle but had to go to the side. I used to help the school cleaner to sweep two classrooms and a length of corridor. The cleaner gave me a penny a week, so I asked some girls who would like to go to church in my place and I would give them my penny. The coveted penny changed hands and I did not go for some weeks until the housemother noticed I had no money for sweets. She said; "isn't it about time your turn came round, Grace?" So I had to go. We had a lovely Vicar called Rev. Wilks. He was a Horticulturist and propagated the Shirley Poppy. When he died two huge beds of Shirley Poppies were planted either side of the administration block. He had a crab tree in his garden and we used to take a tin bath and collect the apples for crab apple jelly. We tasted some but they were much too sour, so we threw it away.

We were taken out of Shirley School to the Shirley Hills to spend a day there. We packed our dinner and tea in a basket and an urn of cocoa. We had to be careful not to spill it as it was very heavy, but we did not mind as long as we went. There used to be a gypsy encampment by the Sandrock Hotel and we would tear past it in case they took us away. The Shirley windmill was a source of wonder to us although it wasn't going. The housemothers used to have a pot of tea. We used to go the cottages in Badgers Hole and ask for some boiling water for a cup of coppers. If we had any money we used to stop at Mrs King's sweet shop. We would buy 16 aniseed balls for a penny or two sherbert bags or liquorice strips or two cats eyes, which changed colour as we sucked them. Sweets were handed round and you were told what colours yours was when it was your turn. Everything was shared.

The Headmaster used to come down to the school every Monday and any boy who had transgressed would be severely punished. All the boys were assembled in the school hall and a vaulting horse was put on the stage. The boy was held on the vaulting horse by a retired Sergeant Major and the Headmaster gave him six strokes with his cane. Their screams would have put a Nazi Torture Chamber to shame. Boys were always running away.

The girls were punished heavily too. We were sent to bed with no tea and all treats like treacle tart and roly-poly pudding were stopped. We were fed but we were always hungry – it was war time.

Leonard came to the school when he was 12 years old. He had spent most of his young life in hospital. He was not happy in the school and spent most of his time running away. He used to wait till it was Friday and then climb up on the boys' toilets and drop down onto Beckenham Golf Course and off and away to spend the weekend with his dad. He did this so often that the Bermondsey Board of Guardians told his dad that they could not keep him anymore. So we never saw him again.

At school we had to write an essay on "Kindness To Animals". I won a certificate and, as it was an all-England effort, Princess Alice, Countess of Athlone, was asked to present the certificates at Crystal Palace. Florrie, my friend, and I were given a new Panama, white gloves and a new dress. We went to the Crystal Palace in the morning and were told to keep clean. We found a blackberry bush and we picked them with our white gloves on and put the blackerries in our new Panama hats. Imagine our horror when we found all the blackberries had stained our gloves and Panamas. The housemother was furious and said we would be the only girls without hats and gloves. It didn't seem to worry Prince Alice one little bit but our day was ruined. I had a seat on top of the organ and it gave me a terrible headache and bilious attack the next day. I won a certificate the next year but we didn't have to go and collect it from any celebrity, which was good for us!

Sports Day was the highlight of our year. We did all sorts of country dancing and the little ones danced the Maypole. I came second in the girls' championship and I won a silver watch. We ran at Stamford Bridge, Chelsea, in the Inter-Schools competition. There was a girl in Birch Cottage who was very fast. She was not well on the day and they took me as first reserve. She decided she would run on the day and, of course, lost the race. I was terribly disappointed.

We had swimming galas as well and we were taught to dive in the pool with all our clothes on, boots as well, and practice four different methods of lifesaving, which came in useful for my badge when I was in the Guides.

Farmer Still's fields backed on to us and there were cows and lovely buttercup fields. I can still see them yet. Farmer Still's daughter wanted to form a Guide troupe so she came down to the school classrooms and asked who would like to join. I shot up my hand and my name was taken down. I did not realise I would have to wear a uniform until I was told to report to the needleroom. The staff duly measured me and sent the uniform to the cottage, much to my pleasure. But the housemother was furious because she was not consulted and she made my life a misery because of it.

I enjoyed being a Guide. We went camping to Cooden Beach. We had never seen the sea before, so we thought you had to go down steps like in our swimming pool. We were terrified and would not go near it. When we were on cooks' patrol, we had to cook some dried apricots. We had never seen them either, so we ate some raw and were terribly sick. I can't look an apricot in the face even now.

We learnt a bit of Latin and grace before dinner, it went like this: *Non nobis Domine non Nobis, Sed Nomine tuo de gloriam, Sed Nomine tuo de gloriam, Non nobis Domine.* When translated it read: Not unto us oh Lord, Not unto us, but unto thy name give the glory.

The children's relations were allowed to visit, but no children were allowed in. The Armed Forces were the exceptions. My brother Frederick came in hospital blues and khaki. He lost a button and I found it on the floor and wanted to take it and show the girls but he said he would get into terrible trouble if he appeared on parade without it. He gave me a choice of a shilling which he said I could spend on sweets so I took the shilling and gave him back his button.

Eventually my brother stopped coming and I learnt very much later that he had died of wounds in Gallipoli. His wife came on a day which was not a visiting day and brought with her a little girl of six years and a baby in her arms. The officials would not let her in and I had to talk to her through the gate.

A girl named Violet came to live in Beech. She was about ten years old and was German and was not accepted because of her nationality. She was very unhappy and became incontinent as a result. She had to wear a ring of cotton reels round her waist at night and

when the housemother went to bed at 10.30 pm they used to tip the mattress up with Violet on it onto the floor and the poor child had to remake the bed in the freezing cold. There was no heating in the bedroom. She had to stand at the corner of the road where all the children went to school with a long-handled broom and wet sheets over her head. Then she had to take the wet sheets to the laundry which was a good half mile away and was deliberately made late for school, for which she got the cane again. My heart bled for her. She was never allowed to go out to play, but was given a task to do until it was bedtime.

One Saturday morning, the housemother was in a particularly bad mood and made all the children do their set tasks twice over. Violet was responsible for cleaning the linoleum hallway floor, which you could see your face in. She had to do it again and polished under the mat. Doctor Ridley used to come round on Sundays to see that we were all well. He was a pompous man but quite kind. He stepped on the mat and went flat on his back. He was furious with the housemother which of course came back on Violet. A large notice came round to all the cottages: "Do Not Polish Under the Mats". We wanted to laugh but dare not.

One evening Violet had all the boots and shoes to clean and was crying bitterly. So I said "What's the matter, Violet?" She said "I don't feel well". She was terrified to tell the housemother, so I told her. The housemother said "Since when have you been a trained nurse? Perhaps you would like to take her up to the infirmary?" This was at least half a mile by road and when we got there she was put in isolation. The next day she was transferred to Shooters Hill fever hospital with Scarlet Fever. Leastways it gave her a respite from that cruelty. But Violet had the last laugh. The Government were giving assisted passage to Australia for £10. She took advantage of this and went to Australia. She married a sheep farmer and had two lovely boys and she was not incontinent any more. It gives me great pleasure to be able to recount this.

When I was 14 years old I left the classroom to begin training for the outside world. We had to make a complete wardrobe when we were in the needleroom, including a winter outdoor coat. I hated sewing and did not give of my best. It was because we had sewing and knitting during the school years and I was chosen to make a night dress for the matron to go on exhibition. The ink wells were removed and a cover was put over the desk. One afternoon the boy whose turn it was to remove the inkwells forgot. The teacher was not pleased with my sewing and said it was not up to exhibition standard so she took it out and told me to start again. I was so angry and flung the night dress on the desk and the inkwell jumped up and stained the mauve night-dress. I didn't have the courage to tell the teacher and folded it up and put it in my sewing bag. The next sewing session came round and to my horror instead of one blot of ink there were about six where it had soaked through the folds. The teacher said "Why ever didn't you tell me. I might have been able to do something about it. Now it is hopeless. You won't be able to go to the exhibition now". I didn't mind and was greatly relieved to think it was all over, but it didn't enamour me to sewing any more.

At fifteen and a half years old we were sent out to situations as a domestic servant. It was traumatic. We did not have an interview with our future employer before we left. I was sent to Bromley. They collected me in a car and told me how lucky I was to have a ride. My heart was breaking at leaving everything behind. Having come from wide open spaces and everything geared for children I could not understand it and I cried for five days non-stop. They were considering sending me back to Shirley, but the lady's sister came from Dulwich. She was very kind to me and gave me some chocolate so I stopped crying, but had I known they were considering sending me back to Shirley Schools I would have kept on crying.

*   *   *   *   *   *   *   *   *   *   *   *   *   *   *   *   *   *

Florence Waters, nee Smart (1914–26)

I don't sleep much these days, so of course I have plenty of time to reminisce as though it was yesterday about my life at Shirley Schools. We had two cruel housemothers; they were cruel women. I never told anyone this.

I was in this Home in Peckham Rye until I was four. Then the First World War was coming in the August and I had a bald head because I had ringworm. I even remember being under the machine and light. I got ringworm in the babies' home though, before I went to Shirley in 1914.

When I got to Shirley, they made me sit up on a chair. I was only four and I suppose it was because of my bald head. We had to call the staff "Mum" and we had to say good morning and good night Mum. Since then I hated saying good morning and good night, and instead say Hello. Both mothers were spinsters, but Ethel (one of the girls) said (I don't know how she got to know) they always slept together. But being so innocent we never gave it a second thought.

I never had a visitor or any love or anything (laughs). Well, I didn't tell you about these hidings we had. Do you know that's what's wrong – I'm digressing again – there's no spanking these days. Any little thing you do, down would come your pants and they would smack your bum. Both housemothers spanked us for little things; they were really cruel. In the summer we had to go to bed at 6 pm. When we were eight or nine they were glad to get rid of us. There was supposed to be no talking, but you can't lay in bed and not talk, with the sun shining still, so she'd hear it and come and spank us. One night I got out of bed and went into the room to tell them not to make so much noise, but coming back, mother was creeping up the stairs and I just got into bed in time. But I was spanked that night. Another night we were playing "I Spy" next to my bed. But she went to shut me up and I bit her and got the cane as well. I had to stand in this girls room and she forgot I was standing there, so I stayed there until 10pm. At the age of 14 we were allowed to stay up until 9pm.

There were ten of us in the big dormitory and seven or eight in the small dormitory. There were eighteen to a cottage in those days. It must have been difficult all in one room. In those days we were so innocent; we just undressed and never bothered what anyone looked like. Sex was never mentioned. I never saw boys - I didn't know what they were for! I was 19 before I knew where babies came from – that's how innocent we were. Matron Capes, dear little old thing she was, used to give us lectures after we left school. Once a week we had to go to her place. She rumbled on and I never knew a word she was talking about. She said to be careful with the men or you get into trouble; the boys go scot free and you are left with the burden. I thought we were sent to prison. Later, Matron Holmes came, a widow's daughter, she looked down on us "poor little orphans".

We were little kids, of course, but we all had a job to do before school: stairs to polish, cleaning and so on. Breakfast in the winter was a plate of porridge, bread and dripping or bread and jam. You never got butter and jam together. We left the cottage at 8.30am to walk to school, getting there at 9am.

When we were naughty, as a punishment we were sent to bed all day Sunday with nothing to eat. I remember only once someone bringing me a piece of bread. Another punishment was 18 pairs of boots to clean in the cold out-house known as the wash room. Then we had to show them to mother.

I got on all right at school. Although I was pretty clever, I couldn't do sums. I can't add up now, my brain just snaps. We were a mixed class but the boys never bothered me and we never took any notice of the boys. I don't like poetry, but we had to learn it. They made me stand up and recite "Daffodils – I wandered lonely as a cloud that floats on high on the fields and hills".

I adored history and gardening. Anyhow, I rose and got to standard 5 and then we had our exams. I must have passed with good colours because I went straight on to 6. There were so many going to 6, the best ones, who got the highest marks. I was proud of myself. A really good solid education we had.

The recess period was between 12 and 2pm and we went home for lunch. The food was good, but they never cooked afters; there again, it was rice pudding every day. They were too lazy to cook puddings. We only got plum dough, as we used to call it when the relief mother was on duty.

At the age of 13 we walked in crocodile line in our white dresses to the church and celebrations at Easter.

We did have a good Christmas. I must say that they were good to us. We had an apple, orange and sweeties all put in our socks. Who paid for them I don't know. We got a little toy. When I was 13 I still had a teddy bear. We used to take stones from raisins at Christmas and they even made a cake. I stirred a Christmas pudding with sixpence in it. We once had pork for Christmas from the pig farm. I wondered why the pigs were squealing, but they had their throats cut.

I was always in Ash Cottage and had two stays in the infirmary in the twelve and a half years that I was there. The treatment in the infirmary was ok.

We had a damn good education and were looked after. It was just that the housemothers were so cruel to us and with my nature, I thought I must have done something wrong to deserve the treatment. I was a 'tom-boy' and always getting into scrapes. Another thing they used to make us do, we had to show our knickers every night to see if we had messed or wet them.

On Saturdays they used to let us go to Croydon to do any shopping. The first time I went there, was when I left elementary school. Not that I had any money from the time I was born until I earned my first £1 0s 7d a month doing domestic work.

The housemothers used to gamble a lot. I'd had a half a dollar sent to me and half a crown given to me by another old school chum that had left. I was robbed by the housemothers of five shillings. All our lockers were robbed to make money for their gambling. They used to nick all the food and sell it. Oh, they were a couple of wicked women, and when they got the sack, they bought a bungalow in Shirley, and damn me if Ethel didn't go and work for them. I have remained friends with both Ethel and her sister June who was also in Shirley and have had regular contact.

We left school at 14, but not until after we had our first period. I didn't know my birthday until then. I was about to leave when the Headmaster told me the actual date, 26 August 1910. Before this I used a date in November.

Then we had three months housework training, three months laundry work and ironing. We were taught needlework for three months and how to wash. I won a silver cup while being taught how to iron. My teacher brought me one iron and I said it wasn't hot enough, and put it on my tongue. It burnt me so I deserved that cup. After three months learning cookery, I left Shirley Schools on 26 March 1926, aged 16 and a half, and went into domestic service in Streatham. I was then employed at Kennards Department Store for a period of two years and then moved onto Selsdon Park Hotel as a waitress.

Despite the cruelty, I was happy going on in my childish way, with much floating along. I didn't know any better. I was young and healthy.

However, I have no regrets. I am not bitter, and have taken the best from the experience.

*   *   *   *   *   *   *   *   *   *   *   *   *   *   *   *   *   *   *

Bert Price (the 1920s)
To the best of my recollection, my admission to Shirley Residential School was arranged by a Church of England Minister of Eugenia Rd, Rotherhithe, who approached Bermondsey Borough Council.

I was taken to a house in a turning off Tooley Street where I remember being stripped, given a bath and then dressed in long trousers. The same day I was taken to a large three-storey house, where I stayed for a short period before being taken – apparently free from infection – to the Reception Cottage at Shirley Schools. After another few days I was again announced free of infection and sent to a proper cottage, Walnut Cottage.

Once we got into a routine it was easy-going, except for those coming into care after 10 years old. They had experienced 'freedom' on the outside and took ages to settle.

I don't know the exact figures, but there were very few orphans. Those I knew seemed more content than those who had parents; who were always saying, "I wish I could go home". However, we orphans did feel left out on visiting days, when we saw the others receiving sweets and fruit from their parents.

The Headmaster was strict and we were all very subdued in his presence. Anyone who received the cane from him was careful not to do so again. He always stressed that he expected only politeness and good manners to be shown to his staff.

The staff in those days were untrained, but in general were good and kind; very few children ever complained about them. I visited all the cottages, delivering various items, and got to know most of the staff very well. Out of approximately 60, there were only two I would have liked dismissed. We addressed them as 'Miss' or sometimes just 'M'.

Except for the Nursery and Bandmaster's cottages, all the other cottages were supervised by one woman, who looked after 14 to 16 children. She usually kept most things under control. Any serious infringement of regulations was reported to the Headmaster, who resorted to the cane when he considered it necessary. There was also a senior matron and an assistant matron who had the responsibility of dealing with bad girls.

My first Housemother was Miss Marshall; she was simply wonderful. She would join us for breakfast each morning wearing her red and white vertically striped dress, and the same at dinner time. When she returned for Tea, she would be in her black dress with a white pinafore – she looked smashing day after day.

I don't remember her smacking anyone, and she never raised her voice when she told us off. We bragged about how good she was to us. Then she retired.

Next came Miss Goddard. We were lucky again. She was just like Miss Marshall, but more motherly. She taught us to dance and the under sevens always had a kiss and bedtime story before going to sleep. She too was wonderful, but died of cancer.

As you can guess, I was happy and content, even though I had no visitors, but it was not long before I wanted to run away – where to, I don't know! Fortunately I was 14, so I asked the senior matron for a transfer to the Bandmaster's cottage. It was arranged that same week, and was the start of another happy period with Mr Parr, the Bandmaster, and his wife. The cottage was known as Laurel Cottage, and was considered for senior boys only. I stayed under their care until I left to take up a job away from Shirley Residential School.

Our schooling was below average. I think there were ten teachers, who came in daily and taught us the three R's. Once we reached 11 we were in the top class and, for three years, until we were 14, our education was at a virtual standstill. If any children showed ability, they were given extra lessons to prepare them for grammar school. If suitable, we were able to attend music classes with a view to joining the school band. This was my choice.

We had a great band, and were invited out to appear at various functions; such as school sports days, Mayday Hospital, Croydon fêtes etc. The Bandmaster would pay us. This was in addition to the 3d per year boys who did not have relatives received in pocket money. When I had saved enough money, the Bandmaster took me to an optician in London Bridge, where I purchased a pair of horn-rimmed glasses. I was so pleased.

Every so often, on Saturday morning, the band paraded around the grounds of Shirley Schools, to the delight of the children. Many of the boys who played in the band went on to join the forces when they were 16.

At 14 we left classroom schooling and were given an opportunity to learn a trade or skill. The tutors came in daily. The girls could choose between needlework, laundry, cooking, domestics or nursery, and the boys, engineering, boot repairs, tailoring, carpentry, plumbing, gardening or the grocery trade.

I chose grocery. I was taught to cut meat, weigh items, check stocks and delivery. I had to ensure the quantities available covered the allocated amount per head. It was during my grocery training that I visited the cottages with the milkman or the baker and got to know the staff so well. It is also why I have such clear memories of the cottages.

The cottages except for the toddlers cottages had two-bedded, five-bedded and seven-bedded rooms. There were also two cottages, Honeysuckle and Ivy, which were reserved for hospital patients. A doctor visited each day, and a dentist once a week.

Each cottage was kept perfectly clean by the children, who were taught dusting, scrubbing, cleaning knives and forks, peeling potatoes, making beds etc, and the housemother did the cooking. Each morning, at 6 am, the hooter sounded, and by 7 am the upstairs room had to be cleaned and the children washed, dressed and ready for breakfast.

Our meals were simple. Breakfast was two slices of bread and dripping, and in the winter a basin of porridge with a cup of cocoa. Tea was two slices of bread with jam or treacle, and on Sundays we had currant bread. Our main meals were Sunday - roast Monday - Shepherds Pie; Tuesday - soup; Wednesdays - roast; Thursday - stew; Friday - sausages, and Saturday - soup. There was always a pudding, rice, tapioca, jam or currant roll. At Christmas we also had Christmas cake, fancy biscuits and an egg for breakfast.

Each child had three sets of clothes, which were stamped with the number of the cottage and then 1 to 16 according to our individual number within the cottage. My number was seven. One set of clothes had to be kept for best and special occasions, such as church and visitors. When I left I was supplied with a large attaché case, three suits, three pairs of shoes, six shirts, vests, pants, handkerchiefs, socks and an overcoat.

We had no wireless or TV sets in the cottages. After we had finished our darning and sewing, we passed the time by reading or playing board games. We were also allowed to go to the sports ground and play various games but at 9 pm sharp, the bugle would sound and the playing fields would clear. We had a swimming pool at the school. Boys swam on Mondays, Wednesdays and Fridays, and girls on Tuesdays and Thursdays.

Our friends were the other children in our cottage or those who we met in the classroom. We never mixed with outsiders, as our trips outside school were always closely supervised by members of staff.

We never went to the theatre but at Christmas, concert parties came to the school to entertain us. Our football and cricket teams used to invite other teams to visit and occasionally we visited their grounds. I remember playing football at Banstead School, Orpington, Hanwell and Islington Central.

Just before my 16th birthday, I had to leave and move into lodgings in Highgate. I started work daily at Scholbreds, Tottenham Court Road, London. I never heard of any other boy or girl being placed in lodgings and work; I can't remember who took me to Scholbreds for my first job. To be honest, I was afraid and did not want to leave the Home.

In some ways the discipline and routine could be compared to army life. It was a case of: do this, do that, come here, go there. I have often wondered if this is why I adapted to army life so well, and enjoyed my army career so much.

* * * * * * * * * * * * * * * * * *

Jessie Northey (the 1920s)

Jessie Northey, wrote an essay describing the holiday she took in summer 1929.

Many of the children who went to camp at Dymchurch, had never before seen the sea. The Mayor of Bermondsey, Councillor George Horwood, JP, offered prizes to the children for the three best written accounts of the visit. Jessie Northey was awarded first prize, Victor Caney the second, and Rose Reynolds the third. This is Jessie's essay:

My Holiday at Dymchurch

On August 23 two hundred and fifty very excited children, laden with kit bags, could be seen scrambling into charabancs, despite the recent orders "Not to scramble", as there was plenty of time. After everybody was comfortable, and the remaining few had said "Good-bye", we started off on the road for Dymchurch.

We had a very interesting ride, passing massive hop fields, the river Medway, and Leeds Castle, which we were informed was recently bought by an American for sixty thousand pounds, and it has a moat round it.

After three and a half hour's riding with only one stop, we alighted from the vehicles in great anxiety to see our residence for a fortnight. It was a long narrow hut, partitioned down the centre. We dumped our respective kit bags at the foot of our beds, and had tea, as the journey had given us wonderful appetites. After tea, we were escorted by Cottage Mothers down to the beach, and paddled. We also sat in a lifeboat, while the captain explained all the works, and showed us some flares which are used when it is dark to signal the crew and any volunteers who would like to lend a hand.

We went on the pier, and watched a diver go under the sea. Several of our girls spoke to him through the telephone, and it was surprising how distinct his voice was. He brought up some very pretty shells as souvenirs. We also saw a model of a coal mine in motion, and it was very interesting indeed; it was with very reluctant feet that we stepped on to the charabanc to go back to camp again.

The smallest public railway in the world went quite close to our camp, and we went from Dymchurch to Hythe on it to see a circus. We were afraid to sneeze lest it should give way. All these events thrilled us so, and the days were slipping quickly by.

The Thursday before our return, four of the men staff decided to provide a miniature concert on the sand. It turned out a great success, and everybody's sides ached with shouting for all we were worth, because we felt so happy. We then returned to the camp, and had a good wash, and so to bed, and to sleep with contentment written all over our faces. We awoke in the morning as fresh as daisies, for we all had a good night's sleep; we washed, and had eight o'clock breakfast, and spent the rest of the morning in the cool but salt sea. After a brisk rub-down we donned our cool garments, and had a welcome lunch, as the sea air had already doubled our appetites. In the afternoon we bathed again, and made sand castles which looked real. We then had tea, and romped in the fields for a short time, had a good wash, and retired to bed at 8pm tired out.

The following few days were just the same, and we were getting browner and browner. We played three netball matches against other schools, and all were very good games. The boys played several football and cricket matches also. The two Sundays we were there we had open-air services, and our band had the honour of providing the necessary music.

About 30 boys and girls went to Folkestone, laughing all the time during the ride. Quite a number of cars stopped on the main road because they were attracted by the shrieks of laughter and the music.

We all slept our last night on camp beds, feeling sorry to have to come home, but we were thankful for the weather we had, because, with the exception of one slight shower, it was faultless. "All good things come to an end", we thought, as we once again got into the charabancs – but not so eagerly this time. The charabancs were soon set going, and, after giving three hearty cheers for the staff at the camp, who were very kind and obliging to us,

we commenced the homeward journey.

We returned by the same route as we came, and this time we saw quite a number of hop-pickers at work. When we reached our own gates we gave three more hearty cheers to let everybody know we were home. Thus came the end to fourteen perfect days.

* * * * * * * * * * * * * * * * * *

Thomas Turner (1926–1939)

My brother Charlie and I were sent to Shirley Schools after our father died. I was 8 months old, and Charlie was two years older. On reflection, the schooling and discipline gave us a good upbringing, but never prepared us for living in the outside world, or in a family. When we returned to live with our mother and sisters many years later, we found it bewildering.

My mother visited on Sundays, when she could afford the shilling fare from Westminster. However, I had no idea she was my mother – or even what a mother was – I just thought she was a kind lady who bought me sweets. I have bitter memories of waiting

Thomas Turner (left) and brother Charles

for her visits. With each call from the Lodge I became more and more jumpy. When my name was called, I had to be inspected and, on many occasions, was sent back to comb my hair or clean my shoes. Not only was this unnecessary, it also shortened the visiting time.

I remember my sister visited one Sunday, but Mr Coombs, the Lodge Keeper, would not let her see us because it was the Sunday we went to church. Mr Coombs was an ex-sergeant major and had lost his leg in the First World War. His attitude over this incident made me dislike him.

I lived in Musk Cottage with 15 other boys, initially with Mrs Hamm as Housemother, and later with Mrs Saunders', whose husband worked at the Lodge, but had no dealings with the boys in Musk Cottage.

When Mr and Mrs Saunders arrived, they brought with them a gramophone. We had never heard a record being played before, and used to listen outside their sitting room to the music. One tune I remember was "Roll Along Covered Wagon". Mr Saunders was the first person I ever saw smoking a pipe. When I asked him about it, I found out he smoked Long Tom or it may have been Tom Long.

We had to learn various tasks, such as darning and cleaning our shoes. Our darning, mending and sewing was inspected by the Housemother, and if it wasn't satisfactory, she put her finger through the darn and made it worse than before. One of the many jobs I disliked was cleaning the knives and forks with brick dust. This was done in the outhouse and was very cold in winter.

On alternate Sundays we went to church and then for a walk, crocodile fashion, to Shirley Hills or West Wickham, where we were allowed to spend our pocket money, which was kept in a cash box and distributed by our cottage mother. The money came from our visitors, so, children who had no visitors had no money. We usually bought sweets and a 1d stamp to write home.

Each Tuesday evening in the winter, we were shown films in the school hall. They always caused great excitement. Our favourites were Cowboys and Indians, the star being Tom Tyler.

When children were 14 years old, they learnt a trade to prepare them for leaving school and going to a situation. We had our own workshops, a large farm and our own water works. (At one time, Croydon and surrounding areas had some sort of typhoid illness due to the water, which I believe caused many deaths. Shirley Schools were not affected owing to having their own system.)

We always knew when a boy was leaving to go to a situation – he left the workshop wearing long trousers and carrying an attaché case.

We had our teeth inspected regularly by a German dentist, who said to each boy: "Open wide, Tommy". As this was my name, I wondered how he knew it.

I can't remember what food we had, just that we had three good meals a day and I usually ate it all. I remember my brother had the job of laying the fire and cutting the bread for breakfast each morning.

We were punished for bad behaviour, such as playing about, being out of bed or talking after lights out. This sometimes meant being locked in the airing cupboard or missing the weekly film. Mr Coombs, the Lodge-keeper, was called in to administer severe punishment for things such as scrumping in the orchard near the entrances or the private gardens which surrounded the playing fields, or for running away. We had to drop our trousers and were whacked with such force we were propelled forward.

I remember being in a play which I think was called "The Woodchopper and his Wife". I played the woodchopper and Jessie Hawkins, who had ginger hair, played my wife. At one point in the play, a sausage-shaped balloon had to end up on my nose. This was done by a boy being held aloft by two ropes, and at the right moment he had to manoeuvre it down, which was then grabbed by me and put on my nose, aided by elastic, which went around my head. This caused a lot of laughter – especially at rehearsals.

My brother Charlie was very good at most forms of sport. I still have the medals he won for the tug of war in 1935 and boxing in 1937. The boxing medal is the size of a 10p and is for the Amateur Boxing Association for eight and a half stone. The tug of war medal is a light and dark blue shield in enamel, and the silver lettering is CSAA.

I remember some of the teachers. Mr Buckingham was Headmaster, then there was Mrs Buckingham, Mr Gibson, Mr Arnold, Mr Westcott and Mrs Boots. I also remember going on holiday once. A fleet of charabancs came to the school. Some of us went to Dymchurch and some to Walton-on-Naze. I went to Dymchurch, and we camped out in bell tents.

My brother and I left Shirley Schools in 1939, just before the war, because my two sisters were old enough to work. My mother moved into a new flat and after the council officials had inspected it, we were allowed home.

The discipline and routine we had in Shirley Schools did stand Charlie and myself in good stead, as Charlie was a commando in the War, and I eventually followed in his footsteps when I was 18.

Older boys from about eight years on, would have a younger boy to look after. They would be shown how to make their beds, wash themselves, fold their clothes and, during our mending sessions, the older boy would have the young one sit with him to be shown how to sew on buttons and darn. In turn, as he grew older, would have a young one to train.

In the front and back of Musk Cottage, there was a bridge. I remember it as being very old, and it spanned ditches. The walls, if I recall right, were about 4ft high and made of bricks fused together, obviously bricks which had lined a furnace. When there was plenty of water in the ditches, we would fish for tiddlers. I recalled this as I took my own grandson to a local park to catch tiddlers and put them in a jam jar.

We looked forward to going to school on Mondays as. after the weekend, there were some golf balls to find which had landed in the playground.

* * * * * * * * * * * * * * * * * *

William Charles Mason (1930–39)

In 1930 my mother died and my father was left with five children aged two to 15 years. It was an era of depression and, apart from this personal tragedy, life was difficult for everyone. For reasons which I shall never know, we were obliged to leave our home in Battersea. However, a kindly couple, friends of the family who had moved a short while previously to Sydenham, offered us shelter. We stayed with them for a short while but, with two daughters of their own, it was crowded, to say the least! The father of the two girls asked the local council for assistance. They in turn, contacted the LCC, and shortly afterwards they were able to admit us to the Shirley Residential Schools.

Unfortunately, my brother, at 15 years, was considered too old for admission and my sister was put into a nursery, a conversion of a pair of cottages named Heather and Hazel. My youngest sister stayed there until the age of six, when she joined her sisters in Chestnut and Daisy. I remember in the receiving house my oldest sister, no doubt in an effort to cheer us up, sang 'Home Sweet Home', but this, of course, reduced us all to floods of tears. Even now, after 69 years, I can still shed a tear for that moment.

The housemother in Violet and Thistle Cottage was Mrs Moore, a gentle soul as I remember her, but prone to having favourites, two of whom coincidentally played saxophone in the school band (it may be that she liked music). I also met an older boy who was a power of strength to me. He was Leonard Arlington who, with his elder brother Edward, came from the Borough of Edmonton in North London. Leonard had the gifts of storyteller and comforter, and I shall never forget him. When Mrs Moore retired, she was succeeded by a number of temporary housemothers. I was transferred after a while to Musk and Myrtle Cottage, where I stayed until the outbreak of the Second War in 1939.

Daily, before school, we were given tasks according to our capabilities: sweeping, scrubbing, washing, polishing, which included a large outside toilet with stone floors and a coal cellar. Inside the cottage we cleaned the lavatories, washrooms, bathroom, stairs and linoleum floors – there was plenty to do.

The evenings were taken up with reading the latest comics – *The Rover, Hotspur, Champion, Wizard* and *Adventure*. More serious reading was obtained from the local library at Ashburton. I have always enjoyed, and still do, the adventure type: *Moore of Corunna* or *Wolfe at Quebec*. Other activities included the board game Ludo, listening to the wireless and crystal set, with its cat's whiskers, hearing music from the great bands of the day.

Father, who worked as a diver for the electrical firm GEC, was unable to visit very often but on one occasion he brought with him an elderly lady, dressed completely in black – a bombazine dress with jet bangles and beads, a large black Edwardian hat and high button boots. She looked to me the epitome of elegance. This lady was in fact my paternal grandmother, and that was the only time I saw her. I recall the over-powering smell of oranges and dust in the band room where visitors and children would meet.

Apart from the normal 'three Rs' elementary education, there were sports in season, stool ball and netball. The head-teacher was Mr Buckingham. His wife was a general teacher and gave classes in elocution. If you mumbled, you were likely to get a child's wooden block in your mouth. The deputy head, Mr Arnold, was a big man, six foot tall, a gentle man and a World War veteran. He was easily diverted from lessons to reminisce about the war. He was sports master and took charge on school journeys. He was able to spot a future raconteur in classes.

We enjoyed educational school journeys. Based at Walmer in Kent, we travelled to historic sites like Canterbury Cathedral, Folkestone, Walmer and Dover Castle.

We also went on natural history visits to ponds and fields. Later, when Mr Instrel had taken over the running of the school in 1934 from Mr Small, we were able to go further afield and given more freedom of movement, based on our honour. He arranged visits to places of interest like the Science Museum, National Gallery, Tower of London and Hampton Court Palace. Later, we went to the Ford Motor Works at Dagenham. On our return, we were to write a competitive essay on what we had seen and heard. When the essays had been judged by an agent of Fords, we were taken to Fords in Croydon, where the winner was awarded a cricket bat autographed by the England team.

When older, we were allowed to go beyond the local area and on one occasion, with a few cronies, we walked to Biggin Hill aerodrome, a distance of about eight miles as the crow flies. After having looked at some of the aircraft, we walked all the way back, another eight miles to Shirley. At other times we joined a crocodile of children and walked to the Addington Hills carrying baskets of food and great urns of tea for a picnic and picking blackberries in season.

Under the charge of Mrs Boots, plays and choirs were set up. I was once lead in 'Robin Hood', but was not destined for the stage, and the following year was relegated to the rear ranks of the spear carriers.

I remember helping to pluck chickens at the farm in preparation for Christmas. Mr Bickley and Mr West were responsible for the farm. Most of the provisions were supplied by the LCC via local contractors to the food stores, whence it was delivered by horse and cart or hand barrow, sometimes by senior boys, to the various cottages. The horses were huge shires, beautiful animals, stabled alongside the lodge at the main entrance. Beside the stables was a magnificent Victoria plum tree, many a plum I scrumped there. Lovely. The manager of the food store was Mr Lowe.

In 1937 we changed from gas to electricity and I remember being plastered with mud while helping Spider Kelly and his gang dig the channels for the cables. Older pupils received training for the future. I was quite adept at metalwork and Mr Steele taught carpentry. I was always able to use my hand in that direction.

Apart from the early years of my stay we were all treated generously and given shelter, food and all available amenities. Shirley was the star of the group of schools run on a similar basis. But for all the generosity, it never equalled the love of a family. It was a beacon of its time and I know I would not have benefited in this way had I not been at Shirley Residential Schools.

Barbara Wells (the 1940s)

In the summer of 1946 or 1947, my two sisters, brother and I were put into care from a court order. This was our mother's second chance (for our moral protection). We were put into Shirley Residential Schools, Wickham Road, Shirley, Croydon.

At the time, Mr and Mrs Instrell were in charge. They were tough and strict. We had a housemother and staff. There was a baby nursery as well as a sick bay, and the dentist came too. Our youngest sister wasn't there very long. She went to foster-parents at Southend.

We went to church at St John's in Shirley, where I attended Confirmation classes. On Friday evenings we went to guilds. I used to do the potatoes by hand and wash veg. in the

Barbara Wells, (left), friend, and Gorden Ali (right)

evenings, get the kids quietly up in the morning, make their beds, mop and bumper the dormitories with polish, all before breakfast.

One little lad always wet the bed, and whether it was summer or winter he had to take his sheets to the laundry. The food was alright, the staff would do big plates of dripping for breakfast and my sister would pinch a plate and bring it up to the dormitory so we could eat at night. Our sweet ration was liquorice all-sorts. We had our boyfriends who would be let in at night and down the drain pipes to go back to their cottages (we were so innocent).

The night watchman reported lights on in our cottages one night, and we were nearly caught. We had the beds across the door and the counterpanes draped over the side of the beds. We told the night staff not to worry and she went back to bed. We went scrumping. We had pocket money, it went up in age. I think the little ones used to get 2d or 3d and so on.

We could go out on Saturday afternoon shopping to Croydon. My brother went to foster parents and when I was 14 I went to my brother's foster-family relations. I liked my outside school. Domestic and cooking were my favourite subjects until my brother picked and picked at the Christmas cake I made, which had to be iced; hence it didn't get iced.

There was always another home on holiday with us; usually it was Banstead Boys, and did our girls love them. It was tears and more tears when we had to come home.

Being in foster-care was fine, but I still missed the Home. Not like today; 40 years ago if you mentioned you lived in a Home, you had a stigma, like being a naughty child. People never think the parents were to blame for you being in a Home.

Somewhere along the line we were taught discipline, manners, and respect for others as well as how to care. Our clothes consisted of three of everything. The summer dresses were pretty.

Bob Wells (the 1940s)

I was in Walnut Cottage, and my sisters in the adjacent cottage called Willow, which was for girls and mine was for boys.

The only housemother I remember was Miss Rogers, a vivacious ginger-haired woman, old to us children of that time but, on reflection, very pretty and at times very quick-tempered. I recall her asking me questions about one of the builders. She had a big crush on him. I think he was Polish. She would send me out with little notes.

I recall going to day-school in Shirley Homes. We had a Mr Gibson as Headmaster and his wife Mrs Gibson was a teacher at the day school. Mr Arnold was a history teacher, not that I learned much about history, because he told us a lot of stories about himself, always an interesting teacher we liked to listen to.

Some of us boys and girls liked to smoke. We managed to get by pinching them out of the staff pockets or the staff in the cottage behind us. I think that was Rose Cottage. When we got caught, we got six of the cane – probably six of the best. We very rarely saw chocolate, but it was always kept in the staff sitting room. Two of my sisters, Barbara and Sylvia, would pinch the chocs and digestive biscuits.

For our sweet ration I think we used to get four toffees a week. We had our pocket money of course; mine was 6d per week. We could go out on Saturdays and mostly went to Woolworths in West Wickham, or sometimes Kennards in Croydon.

At Shirley I started to play the cornet with Mr Parr in charge, who was an extremely pleasant person.

* * * * * * * * * * * * * * * * * * *

John Miller (1946–59)

My sister, Carol, and I were sent to Shirley Residential Schools when I was two and she was a year old. Our first cottage was Holly, where all the very young children were sent, particularly as the nursery was almost attached to it. I have two memories of Holly, one is that at 'potty time' we would be sat on them, shiny metal ones, moving around the floor. The other memory is of being made to eat some vegetables I didn't like – spinach, I think – and seeing a mouse run across the floor. There was a lot of shrieking and standing on chairs by the staff.

Briar Cottage and Cherry were two cottages attached, with an adjoining door, where there was a shared telephone. The cottage had a large dining room at one end of the cottage and a sitting room the same size at the other; between the two was a long corridor with the kitchen, stairs and steps down to the front door on one side. The washrooms had a couple of basins and a toilet in each, the floor

was polished granite, which was freezing in the winter and was used as punishment when we had been particularly naughty. All the floors, apart from the kitchen, were covered in very good quality hessian-backed linoleum, deep red and highly polished, with the exception of the washrooms, bathrooms and stairs. On the left hand side were two washrooms for each sex, and another corridor to the back door, where two bathrooms had been added in the early 1950s.

We always looked forward to Aunty Mary's days off, when she went out to visit her family, as we could get away with things when she wasn't there, like staying out and up later, or getting away with some of the chores. On Aunty Mary's day off, she would play games of postman's knock and I always felt she was looking for me, so I made absolutely sure she wouldn't find me.

The laundry was collected from each cottage on a different day of the week, which also coincided with changing bed linen and towels. Laundry was collected in large bags and stored in the washrooms by the children. It was collected by the handyman who drove around Shirley on a tractor and trailer; he would also deliver the clean laundry. Any repairs to our clothes were done in the needle room, which wasn't attached to the laundry but in another part of the Home, near the school.

Behind Chestnut and Daisy there was an overgrown area of shrubland, with lumps of concrete and bricks from some old buildings. Presumably the original cottages of Chestnut and Daisy were destroyed in the Second World War. The long grass, shrubs and trees we called the 'piggery', which it may have been at one time. My friends and I spent many hours exploring it, playing Cowboys and Indians in it. I was once caught by an arrow fired by the Indians. It was another of those occasions when I went running for solace – this time I needed the arrow removed from my bum.

There were rats to be caught and bludgeoned to death, ants and wasps nests galore. I can remember that on another time I needed to run home, as I was covered in wasps. I was thrown into a bath of cold water. Across the road from the piggery was a small orchard, which in the early years was fenced in, but later, like many fences, they were taken down.

I can vividly remember my class at school all sitting on the floor in the main hall, ready for a games lesson. We were listening to the radio telling us how we should sit straight and not be bent like bananas, when there was an interruption for a news flash to say that the King was dead. The rest of the day the radio played solemn music.

The school playground was quite big, with a very large corrugated shed roof, big enough to hold games when it was raining. Surrounding the playground was a large, long wooden fence, which was also the boundary of Shirley

Shirley's soccer first team with John Miller sitting second right in the first row

Oaks. On the other side was a large park. In the early years this was our only place to look out, and sometimes go outside the Homes to meet other people. If we heard anyone walking along the path that went alongside the fence, we would throw a ball over and most times have some sort of banter with them.

Until I was about ten or eleven, the regime was very strict under the then superintendent, a Mr Instrell. For those of us who were in the Home from an early age, it wasn't obvious until he retired. Corporal punishment was always the first option, and if you were called into the Office, you knew you were in trouble. I had to go twice; I was absolutely petrified, and on both times I was caned, not for any misdemeanours in Briar Cottage, but for being caught in 'out of bounds' places like the orchard. You were made to stand in the corridor outside Mr Instrell's Office. The lady in the Office would smile at you but you knew you were in trouble from her face. After what seemed like a long time, Mr Instrell would call you in. He already had the cane in his hand as you entered the room. I cried on both times, not from the pain but from fear. Children from other cottages were sent to him, some regularly, by their housemothers, either because they couldn't handle them, or because the children couldn't cope with the strict discipline. Some would abscond; these were usually the older ones who were only at the Home for short periods.

There was a general feeling of freedom as we got older. We were allowed out of the Home unchaperoned. Aunty Mary would take us to places of interest during school holidays, like London and Chessington Zoo, the Odeon Cinema in Croydon, plus pantomimes and shows in London, where I recall seeing Winifred Atwell and the King Singers, who were big at the time.

During my time at Portland Road Boys Schools, I represented the school and South Croydon at football, being trained by the youth team coach Jesse Willard from Crystal Palace FC, who was also responsible for training and organising sports at Shirley Oaks. I played cricket for the school as Captain, and was nominated to have trials for the Surrey Schools side. I had my name inscribed on a sports plaque in the school for being the record-holder in both javelin and discus. In my last two years at school I was a prefect, although I believe this was as much to do with my size and being a rough Shirley child, as to do with my lack of academic ability. You could usually pick the Shirley boys at the school, as we were still wearing short trousers until we were at least 13, which caused some problems at the start. These were usually sorted out by us after the punch-ups.

The Home's sick bay was like a mini hospital, without the ability to perform operations. Each day there would be a queue outside of those who were feeling sick and those who required plasters and bandages. We had regular medicals with a doctor who came once a week. It was also the responsibility of the matron to carry out nit parades. I spent a couple of nights there under observation, because I used to suffer regularly from sore throats. I remember the time I almost fainted when they bored a hole through my fingernail to let the pressure off a swollen finger they believed to be infected. It was also where the dentist (I think he must have been a butcher by trade) had a surgery. He too visited weekly. We had to go for a check-up every six months. Most times I would bunk off somewhere else or make sure I was doing something to miss him. It is only very recently that I have overcome my fear of the dentist, 12 years too late.

Mr Parr was the bandmaster, who rode around Shirley on a bike, with his trumpet and sheet music in a briefcase strapped to the bar. I think he always wore a brown suit and a trilby, which he rarely took off, even when playing. I remember him as a friendly man, tall and slim, with thin silvery hair, wearing wire-rimmed glasses. When I started with the band, my first instrument was the drums, first the bass then the side drums. This was followed by the euphonic. It was extremely rare for anyone to be able to read music, so to overcome this, Mr Parr would write the number of the valves to press under every note.

Mr Fincham looked after the main stores situated between the Administration Offices and the Superintendent's house. He was responsible for stocking the stores with products from outside suppliers. The house-mothers would give him a weekly shopping list for general items, then go to the stores during the day if they required something fresh. Milk and bread were delivered daily from outside sources. Coal and coke were also delivered directly to the Home. Although the cottages all had a larder and refrigerator, none had a freezer, so any frozen products, such as ice cream, had to be collected as required by each cottage. This meant that ice cream was only available during the store's working hours, between 9 am and 6 am, Monday to Saturday.

In the Summer of 1959, after I had left school, I worked with Mr Fincham for a short period while I was waiting to go to Merchant Navy School. I did enjoy working in the stores, as I was there for all to see and it gave me great kudos with all the other kids. I was put to work making up the weekly orders, which Mr Fincham and I would deliver in a van around Shirley. He was also available to serve anyone who came to collect. I found him a very pleasant man and very talkative, particularly with all the house-mothers who would come in to pickup food during the day; I think it was a meeting place for them.

One sad aspect for me was that my parents never visited me while at Shirley, on the couple of occasions they were expected, one on open day and the other on sports day.

My recollections of Shirley Oaks and feelings I have for it have changed as the years have gone by. From a shyness to mention it in my teens, added to a very strong need to belong to a family, and now looking back with fondness, thankful that I had such a good upbringing which has benefited me now.

* * * * * * * * * * * * * * * * * * *

Rita Hatch (1947–53)

I came from a family of seven children. My father left home when I was about nine, and my mother, (God bless her soul), was unable to cope with all the children. Money was very tight then and we missed schooling. I don't think we went to school because we hadn't the clothes and shoes to wear.

At the age of about ten years, my brother David, aged eight and I had to go to court. We were taken away from our mum and family.

First we went to Stamford House in Shepherds Bush. I don't remember much about my time there, but I know we both cried for most of the time. We were only there for two or three weeks. Then we were taken by car to Shirley Residential Schools. I remember

going through the Lodge gates, with thoughts of the countryside very much in my mind. On the left there was a nursery and further down the drive, on the right, were orchards. There were lots of open spaces around.

Our first stop was the infirmary where we were thoroughly examined by the doctors and nurses. Then we were taken to a building, which inside resembled a large warehouse, with racks of clothes. Both of us were kitted out with three sets of clothes each to last for the summer months. After this we went to the cobblers, where we were given two pairs of shoes. One pair was for school and the other was for best. In addition to this, we were given a pair of Wellington boots. I thought I was dreaming – I had never had so many clothes at one time. It was always hand-me-downs from my two older sisters.

My first cottage was called Plane. The housemother was Miss Crutchley, who I didn't like very much. I suppose she thought I was a bit dim, and I felt I was always in the wrong, but she let me visit my brother David a lot. He was put in Musk Cottage with Miss Rose, the housemother, who I recall was a lovely lady who liked David.

Some of the kids used to venture into Poplar Cottage. Access could be gained by a door that lead through to each twinned building. At the time it was empty, apart from a very old stylish gramophone which we used to play. This was not allowed, of course, but luckily we didn't get found out. Outside Plane Cottage there was a large tree where we sometimes played. It must have been over a hundred years old.

Throughout my stay at Shirley I went home most weekends. My dad or my sister would pick us up at the Lodge and we made fun of Mr Barker, who was usually on duty (Woof, Woof).

We both went to Shirley County Primary School. Mr Instrell was the Headmaster. I remember Mr Gibson and his wife; they were two of the teachers. My brother and I had a hard time at the school. I didn't know very much as we'd never been to school at home.

After about a year I was put into Birch Cottage. Miss Howe was the cottage mother. I got on well with her, although she was very strict. I think it was because I was the oldest girl in her cottage. She would make some lovely dinners and cakes and she would teach me a little bit of cooking. I would have to prepare the veg. every day. There were 14 children in Birch Cottage – that's a lot of potatoes for an 11 year old to do.

I remember washing all the socks at night and cleaning all the school shoes. In the mornings I would have to help make the beds and dress the small children. At weekends it was housework, with the large bumpers to

Rita and David Hatch outside Plane Cottage

polish the floors and cleaning the brass on the front door.

When I was 11 years old, I started school at Haseltine in Lower Sydenham. There were a lot of us from Shirley who went to that school. We would get a 194 bus to Haseltine at about 8.30 am each day.

Molly Bitmead was one of my best friends at school. She was put into Birch Cottage and we had a great time. Miss Howe would give us pocket money and a bag of sweets. I remember going to the pictures at West Wickham some Saturdays. We would often go to Shirley Hills; it was a smashing place, and a gang of us would go there quite a lot. The swimming pool was another great thing we had at Shirley. We were always in there messing about. Even when the doors were locked, we'd find a way in.

At about the age of 13 I got psoriasis. I was given malt to drink twice a day in the hope it would help. It remained with me until I reached my late 20s.

On Sundays all the school went to Church, which was just up the road, a lovely Church. In the summer, all the kids would clamber on the coaches for a fortnight's holiday at Martello

Tower camping site at Walton-on-the-Naze. We all slept in tents. There was a large hut in the middle of the camp, which was a dining hall. We had a great time there.

If kids were caught scrumping – thank goodness I wasn't – they were punished. The boys would be caned and the girls were kept indoors, deprived of free time.

When I was about 14, one of the teachers formed a bicycle club. There must have been 20 of us in this club, and we would go out in the evenings around West Wickham and Addiscombe. After we'd passed a test of course! We even went to Whitstable that year for a week. The bikes went on a lorry and we went by coach. They didn't trust us to ride all that way.

I remember going to the infirmary one year with chicken pox. The nurses were smashing but I don't remember any of their names.

In the summer we would have sports at Shirley. We all had to do our bit. The Shirley choir sang at the Royal Albert Hall.

I left Shirley in 1953 and lived with my older sister and her husband in the New Kent Road. On leaving Shirley to start work, I was taken shopping in Croydon and kitted out with very smart clothes and shoes of my own choice. My first work was at Debenhams and Freemans doing tailoring. After a year I moved back with my mum to help out with the money – not that I got much of that.

David, my brother, was still at Shirley, so I would go down and fetch him home for the weekend. Plus I would see some of my old mates again.

I met Bob Wells one night while I was out with my cousin Carol on our bikes. Two chaps started to chat us up and I found out that Bob Wells had been at Shirley. I didn't remember him, but I knew his sisters Sylvia, Barbara and Iris from Willow Cottage. Bob had been in Walnut Cottage. We got together and finally were married in December 1957 at Walworth Town Hall. We had three lovely daughters: Yvonne, Christine and Sandra. We now have six grand-children. We were very strict with our girls and they are very independent. I suppose it's the discipline we both had when we were kids. My husband Bob and I have been to a couple of reunions. Looking back, we both had a good start in life, thanks to Shirley. More so the girls; we were taught to look clean and look after smaller children. When our families get together, we often talk about the good old days at Shirley. Lots of fond memories, for me anyway.

*   *   *   *   *   *   *   *   *   *   *   *   *   *   *   *   *   *

Louise Hamer, housemother (the 1950s)

I came to Shirley in 1952 following a brief period of employment looking after what are now termed "children with learning difficulties" in Essex.

Having been brought up in the rural countryside of North East England I was very appreciative of the peace and greenery to which I was accustomed. It was rather like a large parkland area with mature trees, lots of open spaces which were clean and tidy, with gray squirrels in quite large numbers. With the friendly atmosphere I immediately felt I would be happy there, an initial thought which was confirmed throughout my stay at Shirley.

My duties meant that I had to be on duty at Chestnut by about 6.45 am in order to prepare the children for school or nursery. The staff, including myself, took turns on a weekly basis to work in the kitchen, preparing meals for one week and undertaking housework such as polishing floors, dusting andcleaning windows. The next week I would take younger children to nursery. There were two other assistants living in the cottage and this meant that I had to "sleep out" at a house named Aster, which was run by a housemother called Olive Harris, who cared for the older children between the ages of 11 and 16. Olive Harris and I became good friends, a friendship that lasted for long after I left Shirley, until she died some years ago. I stayed at Chestnut for about 18 months, then was given a housemother's job in a single cottage called Laurel.

In their lives at Shirley, the children were encouraged to spend as normal a life as possible by joining the local youth organisations, such as cubs, scouts, guides and brownies. Great importance was placed upon good behavior at Shirley. At weekends we used to go to the park opposite St John's Church and play ball games, weather permitting. The atmosphere at Laurel was very much that of a happy family, it was easy to get very attached to the children. Christmas was a very happy and busy time, some of the children would go and stay with their parents and those that remained at Shirley would go to a pantomime, visit the circus and attend parties. Each cottage was responsible for its own party arrangements and there was always plenty of food and presents for the children.

On Sundays I used to take the children to church which happened to be Church of England. There were children of different denominations in the group but even if they didn't take part in the service, I felt that it contributed to their observance of good behavior, – a feature which was often commented upon by people we met. I suppose that it was a sign of changing times and outlook that during the last year of my stay at Shirley, there were moves to segregate some children of different denominations into separate cottages.

During my time at Shirley I was allowed two weeks personal holiday which I generally used to take with my family in the North East of England. However it is worth mentioning that it was during this period that I had the first real holiday of my life, I went to Wales with my friend Olive Harris.

I enjoyed over five years at Shirley, a period which I often reflect upon as perhaps the happiest of my life but I felt the need for a change and decided to move. All my memories, however, of my stay there are happy ones and I made many lasting friendships, outweighing any regrets that I may have over leaving.

* * * * * * * * * * * * * * * * * *

Gerry Coll (1963–73)
One of my earliest memories was going to the nursery. I can recall the nursery teachers making cakes in the kitchen of Holly Cottage.

I remember the excitement of going on holiday for two weeks – for us, if not for our housemothers. On a Saturday morning, a distinctive sky blue coach with a white roof and the words 'London County Council' along the side in white, turned up to take us away. Every year it would transport us to Margate or Southsea or to one of the mainline stations, such as King's Cross, if we were going to Scarborough. Before leaving the Home, our coach would usually stop at the Lodge, where we would be waved off the premises by Mr Cummings. I formed the impression that this official was a faithful steward to Shirley Oaks. He was generally popular with staff and children alike.

On school assembly mornings, I remember singing hymns like 'Praise my Soul the King of Heaven', 'We plough the fields and scatter' and 'God is Love'. Each class had to sit in neat rows on the wooden blocked floor. The infants sat nearest to the stage with the other classes behind. At either side of the hall, after a small gap, the class teachers would be seated on chairs keeping a watchful eye on their class.

As a junior, I remember the Deputy Head-master, Mr Mott, addressing a school assembly about "the great technological and scientific advances that are being made in our lifetime". He said that, as a boy, he couldn't imagine a plane travelling twice the speed of sound. Mr Mott stated that the biggest miracle of all though was the gift of a new-born baby. After assembly we would file out of the hall down the corridor to our classroom led by our teachers.

One icy winter morning before school started there was a fierce snowball fight between the boys. A girl got caught up in the affray and was struck by a series of snowballs. Mr Mott heard about her distress, identified the culprits and when the school gathered the following morning for assembly, he called the boys involved in the incident to the front of the hall. Instead of giving them a taste of his brown floppy slipper (nick-named the 'Willie Wacker'), he asked the whole school to go out into the front playground. Then he lined the boys a few feet from the school hall wall, and invited the girls to throw the snowballs he had made at them. When he felt justice had been done, he asked the boys how did they like it. They seemed very embarrassed though not actually humiliated. I would like to add that Mr Mott was a well-liked and respected teacher, who had patience and understanding when working with children of less academic ability.

At primary school I was considered 'backward' when trying to learn the three Rs. I loved drawing, art and pottery classes. In my art classes – I think it must have been around 1970 – I built a bomb, made from wood, that resembled a rocket and threatened as a prank to blow up the school. To my disappointment and to some children's amusement the teachers ordered the rocket be dismantled, after I had encouraged a few of the children to collect discarded gun powder from a Guy Faulkes' bonfire!

I recall going to band practice on Wednesday evenings with Mr Parr who gave me individual tuition for a short while. I didn't really take to the trumpet because I could not get enough air into it but Mr Parr had a lot of patience in trying to teach me even though he didn't succeed. He used to wear a trilby hat and ride a black bicycle.

Beside Myrtle Cottage, close to the ditch, were a children's slide, swings and rocking horse where I often played with other kids. In the summer time I used to hear what sounded like a swarm of bumble bees in the distance. It was only later I learned from my housemother that it was motor car racing at Crystal Palace. Another memory I have is the long grass, where we used to meet to play games and where some romantic encounters took place. I can also recollect the sound that the grasshoppers made in the summer.

The open spaces, trees and bushes seemed to make the air fresh. The smell of newly-cut grass made it even more memorable. I remember fields of buttercups and daisies. Occasionally I accompanied my housemother to the Homes' office where the typist, Mrs Crump, was very pleasant, taking time out from her work to give us sweets.

At Christmas time we used to attend numerous parties. My favourite was Mr Wade's party, somewhere in the Pett's Wood area. This was a very popular event as somehow the

A typical 'Cottage' group with Gerry Coll seated second from the right, front row

food and presents were more pleasurable and desirable. I often wondered what link Mr Wade may have had with the Home, though I feel it might have been more with the school.

In the evenings approaching Christmas we were given an assortment of nuts including almonds, walnuts, brazil-nuts and hazelnuts to celebrate the festive season. We also enjoyed large bottles of tizer, ginger beer and coca-cola, usually consumed before going to bed.

Like many children at Shirley my father seldom visited. His absence left me searching for some positive male role models that would give me some sense of security. I'd always loved music and recall how Radio 1 used to fill the cottage dining room most weekends. The first record that played on my mind was the Four Tops' 'Reach Out'. As I grew older I developed a great love for R 'n' B and Gospel music. As a young adult I collected albums by Aretha Franklin, Marvin Gaye, Phyllis Hyman, Stevie Wonder, Otis Reading, Anita Baker, Bobby Womack, Al Green, and the legendary Philadelphian singer Teddy Pendergrass. This year I had the opportunity to read his wonderful autobiography *Truly Blessed*. His courage and determination in the face of great adversity has been a great inspiration to me.

As I grew older I promised myself that if I married or was in a relationship with a woman who already had children, I would not reject or desert them. Knowing the effect not having reliable parents had on me as I was growing up, I was determined not to revisit this on other children. I love children and their well-being is most important – after all they didn't ask to come into the world.

My full-time housemothers were Aunties Barbara and Delia, who some children from other cottages mistook for sisters. They were very close and generally fair-minded with the children, though they could be very strict. Looking back, I see that they tried to instill a sense of pride in us and were very protective, especially of those children who were in their

care for a number of years. They encouraged us to be positive about the present and future and not to be too affected by our past, which I found encouraging .

A few nights every week our housemothers would take turns combing and plaiting two black girls' hair. They would apply vaseline to soften and relax the hair. The girls and their parents were very appreciative of the results. Bearing in mind it was the late 1960s and early 1970s this showed an understanding in meeting the hair care needs of ethnic children from women who were well into middle age. Vaseline was also used for skin care. Jonson's baby oil or emulsifying cream, collected from the surgery by members of staff, was used at bath-time to keep the skin from drying out.

On a weekday evening our clothes would be neatly positioned on the right-hand side of the wooden stairs against the banisters. The youngest child's clothes would be placed on the bottom step and the belongings were elevated on each step according to age, with the eldest child's clothes piled at the top of the staircase. When it was children's bedtime they had to pick up their clothes and carry them up the "wooden hill" to their bedroom.

Father Patrick Best was another person who made an indelible impression on me, as adults often unknowingly do on children. Chaplain to the Catholic children at the Home, he was popular with most of us, even those from different religions. His catechism classes were not about indoctrination but gentle persuasion. This made a lasting impression on me. He would throw pieces of chalk at individual children if he thought they were not paying attention. Later I met members of the congregation of the Daughters of Mary and Joseph who would also have a marked impression on me: Sisters Kathleen, Margaret, Mary Peter, Mary and Sheila.

I remember playing football all the time. I'll never forget one late summer Friday night when I played five- or six-aside under the floodlights behind the school against a group of older boys and won. Some of these boys were bad losers and chased us back to our cottages. Before I reached the age of ten my housemother asked me if I wanted to go to Crystal Palace. I thought this meant a visit to the recreational park. It wasn't until I met up with children from other cottages that I realised I was going to a professional football match. It was the first of many memorable matches at Selhurst, especially the 5–0 thrashing of Manchester United! I remain a keen fan of this colourful club to this day. Back in those early days, after each match we would assist the groundsman, Len Chatterton, on the pitch by replacing the divots and clearing the rubbish from the terraces.

I keep in sporadic contact with Daisy, Doreen, June, Maureen, Pam and Sylvia – the houseparents who used to work at Shirley. I appreciate the many friends I made there, especially Floyd and Raymond (who are brothers), Clay, Clive, Dorothy, Tony and Paul, whose friendship prevented me from being lonely (a loneliness that would isolate me a few years later) and initially helped me to get in touch with my identity. When I moved to Southwark at 16 years of age, I met up with two brothers whose family were extremely good to

me. I am still in regular contact with Rodney and Paul, who I grew up with in Shirley.

Before going to Goldsmiths College, I had the opportunity to work for First Key, an organisation that advocates on behalf of children preparing to leave care. I was working alongside Paul, Carol and Jenny, researching and producing documents for various local authorities. Sometimes it is easy for me to believe that people's lives outside the care system were far better than mine. It wasn't until I had a career working with people that I realised that this was far from always the case. Later, I worked with Victoria Laughland, founder of the *Who Cares?* magazine and the Who Cares? Trust.

Having spent my childhood in institutions, and with adolescence starting to bite, I became very disillusioned and unhappy. I was slowly becoming aware that rather than helping me to prepare for leaving care, I was being encouraged by staff to become even more dependent. Instead of learning to grow away from a protected upbringing I perceived that I was being encouraged to grow into it. My later experience of long term care was very painful. Co-writing this book has enabled me to close a chapter in my life. I now plan to take with me only the good memories I had at Shirley.

* * * * * * * * * * * * * * * * * * *

Raymond Stevenson, Lime Cottage (1966–77)
If we are all a product of our upbringing then a confused, multi-faceted extrovert is the outcome of me, Raymond Stevenson, spending my early childhood in Shirley Oaks.

Of the horror stories that follow most people's existence in institutions as unnatural as a dog bringing up a cat, I have none. Maybe this was because I was seen as someone to be wary of. As a boy I was acutely aware of the dangers around me. I could see other children being dragged into a life of confusion: if they were black, the feeling of a lack of blackness

and no-one around to love them and if they were white no-one around to love them.

As I delve deeper back the memories that rise to the surface first are of aunts and uncles, as they were called, who really cared, who did more than their fair job's worth. I think they had a clear understanding of the emotional support that was needed. Shirley Oaks was an enclosed world that most of its 200 or more inhabitants were led to believe was the only world. Surrounded by a giant perimeter wall from the outside, one could believe that the animals had been safely caged.

100

Like other children I wet the bed. I never really understood why, but I remember I was neither embarrassed nor ashamed. As I search back deeper into my memories, Christmas stands out, as we all believed in Father Christmas. As I grew older and my mind developed I started to rebel. No-one could understand why. I became aggressive, even violent. Screaming for attention, I attempted to burn down the cottage I was living in and the surrounding area. I now realise that however well disguised Shirley Oaks was, it was not my home. Most of the people who worked there were not my protectors. If the truth be known, the job for them was about money. I resented them pretending they cared so my response was to rebel. Looking back, I realise why I survived when so many fell by the wayside. Shirley Oaks made me strong, resilient and amiable to all races. It also made me a loner, a fighter and a survivor. However misguided the care system was, I believe it was the making of me, but I also believe it destroyed other people.

* * * * * * * * * * * * * * * * * *

Paul Noble (1970–83)

I arrived at Shirley Oaks when I was about five years old, in 1970. I lived there with my mum who was working as a care assistant. My first impressions were of wide open spaces, of fields and woods, with children everywhere.

My mum worked in various houses until she became housemother of 'Musk Cottage'. There were around eight children in this cottage. We stayed in this cottage for a few years but then moved to what used to be the superintendent's house, adjacent to the old stores. Throughout my time in Shirley, we kept the name 'Musk'.

There was never a dull moment. Many hours were spent playing 'World Cup' at the football pitch. The games were always good quality, with a lot of good players. One boy, Mark, played for England Schoolboys at Wembley and went on to play for Crystal Palace FC for a while.

When we got bored playing football, the ditch would be the next form of entertainment. The ditch would be dammed up to see if we could stop it flowing. We always failed. There was a swing rope to go from one side to the other. We would get as many children as possible on at one time, trying not to fall into the water, although we often did. The ditch also had a tunnel under the road. It was about 25 metres long. Hours were spent going through the tunnel trying to find rats. We always failed in this task too.

The slide was always used to play 'it'. This game entailed someone running after another child and, if and when they were caught, they became 'it' until they touched someone else. On one occasion I remember being pushed off the top by one of the Stevenson brothers.

There were many clubs to entertain the children. One of the biggest attractions was Mr Hart's Swimming Club on Friday night from five to six o'clock. The swimming pool was in the Engineers' block, and was always busy. Mr Hart was strict. We would swim five lengths front crawl, five lengths back-stroke, and five lengths breast-stroke. Mr Hart would stand on the edge of the pool for one minute, then dive in and swim one length under water. As the years passed by, the numbers attending went from around 35 down to five or six. This was mainly due to the number of children in Shirley Oaks falling until it eventually closed. The kids from Musk Cottage always went. Even in the depths of winter, we would ride our bikes up to the pool. Mr Hart only ever failed to turn up on one occasion.

Mr Hart retired around 1981, the end of an era. In the summer holidays we would go swimming for at least an hour a day. Each cottage would book the pool for an hour.

The summer holidays were great. Days were spent in the orchard, up in the apple and pear trees. When everyone was bored eating, dustbins would be filled with apples. These were taken down to the castle in the piggery, close to Acacia Cottage.

Two teams were picked, usually about 25 children on each side. An apple war would then take place. Many children were hit on the head or in the face, with tears and fist fights likely to follow. One lad nearly lost his eye when hit by an acorn. He had to be taken to hospital.

As we got older, the apples and acorns were exchanged for coal. Everyone went up to the Engineers to the coal bunkers. This was the age of the 'coal wars'. Many a child experienced being hit by a lump of coal, and the occasional window got smashed. These coal wars were usually stopped by the engineers, who would chase us off.

As the 1970s went by, the numbers of children decreased and cottages closed. In the late 70s and early 80s, the days were still spent with bike rides around Shirley. It would normally take $3\frac{1}{2} - 4$ minutes to ride round. Football was still a big part of life, and we would often venture into the allotments for apples and pears, and the odd tomato war.

One of the next big crazes in the Home was go-karts. Everyone would try to find an old pram, usually at the dump in the Engineer s' Block. The wheels would be joined to the plank of wood, with a piece of rope added to steer the trolley. Then we would have go-kart races. Gerry Coll probably had the fastest and biggest, with about six to seven children piling on at one time.

Guy Fawkes' night was always a big occasion. A few weeks before everyone would be looking for dead wood, to see which cottage could make the biggest bonfire.

The children's nursery was another meeting place, with 20 or 30 children playing 'it' on the roof. How no-one ever fell off remains a mystery.

One of the last exciting things I did with Simon, Adrian and Paul, was getting into the Engineers, climbing to the very top of the tower. Once we got to the summit, we had a tremendous view, which could be seen for miles around.

My mum always said "those were the happiest days of my life", looking after many children. For me and many people I have spoken to who were at Shirley Oaks in the years I was there, we could not have found a more enjoyable place to grow up.

*   *   *   *   *   *   *   *   *   *   *   *   *   *   *   *   *   *

Heather Smith-Crome (the 1980s)

I moved to Shirley Oaks in the summer of 1980. As my social worker drove down the long drive towards Violet House, my first instinct was "Oh my God, I'm in the countryside". Everything seemed so quiet and serene. I noticed the beautiful buildings each side of the drive surrounded by green grass, trees and geese!

As we neared Violet House my social worker said "Here we are" and pointed to a group of people lying on the grass. I then began to think that I was in some kind of hippy commune. Several boys in the group had long grass stalks hanging out of the side of their mouths. I especially noticed two women, one being very large and the other wearing a long, flowing dress and a straw hat. My social worker and I got out of the car and walked over to the group. We entered the house and sat down in a large, cool and tidy dining room. The woman wearing the straw hat had now lit a cigarette and was blowing full circles into the air. Introducing herself as Auntie, she then informed me of the basic house rules.

When my social worker had left, a young

girl about the same age as me came into the room. Auntie introduced us to each other, informed her that I was to share her room and could she show me around the house. After being shown all around the building I went back into my bedroom with my friend. She opened her wardrobe and said, "You can borrow what clothes you want of mine, until you get yourself sorted out". This made me feel honoured because she had the most fantastic taste in clothes. We were both exactly the same size and height. From that point on we became best friends. We shared the same interests, had similar personalities and even had the same rare blood group.

In the evening all the children and members of staff sat around a large table in the dining room to eat our evening meal. My friend sat next to me and every so often looked at me and smiled. I felt embarrassed because I had never eaten in front of so many faces before. After dinner we each did our chores and then all the children went into the living room to watch television. I sat in the dining room reading a magazine, still feeling a little uncomfortable. Suddenly, I heard an unusual noise. I looked up to see a strange, large, black creature fly through the window and land on the floor. I got up, looking at it in disbelief because I had never seen anything like it before. I went into the living room to inform everyone about this strange creature. Immediately the boys jumped up shouting "Stag Beetle" and ran into the dining room. There was much commotion as one boy tried to catch the beetle in a long tube without a bottom and it fell out, causing the boy holding the container to scream and jump up and down. Eventually, a man came into the room and said in a loud Jamaican accent, "What's all your problem?" Everyone shouted at once "Uncle, help!". Other children were pretending they were not scared. The boys then returned to the living room to finish watching football. My friend looked at me and said: "Don't worry, they are normally worse than that".

In Violet House we had lots of rules, which generally everyone obeyed because your punishment was 'grounding' – you were not allowed out for unlimited time and you had to do your house chores. If we left our room untidy, when we returned home from school, we would find our belongings piled up like a mountain in the middle of the bedroom. So it was easier to do it right the first time. One of the rules was we had to wear full school uniform, including flat, black, loafer-style shoes. Sometimes my friend and I would sneak our fashionable shoes into carrier bags. When we got past the main entrance to Home and arrived at the bus stop across the road, we would change into our shoes, only to see our uncle pull up in his red car, motioning to say: "Give them to me now". This practically reduced us to tears because no matter how clever we were getting our shoes out of the house, we would always get caught.

One Saturday my friend and I went to visit my parents who lived in Clapham. While waiting for the bus to return to Shirley Oaks, a man came up to us and said,"There are no buses running, there is a riot in Brixton". We didn't know what the word 'riot' meant, so we decided to walk to Brixton to catch the bus home. When we got there we soon learnt the meaning of the word! Hours later we reached Violet House and were in extreme trouble not only because we were late, but had acquired a number of brand-name garments too.

The summers were fun, not only because there was no school, but because we went on holiday together. A memorable time was when we all went to Windsor for a week to experience living on a canal boat. One afternoon my friend and I were sunbathing, when I made a decision to do a long jump across the open hatch to the other side of the boat. I shouted to my friend "Watch me" and fell straight down the open hatch into the kitchen area of the boat. Landing on my back, I looked to see everyone peering down laughing at me and exclaiming 'Superwoman'. Days later I tried to move the boat away from the lock wall and someone pushed me out of the way. I lost my balance and fell into the water – with the water rising and the lock gates closing. Luckily, a man grabbed my arm and lifted me out of the water. All the children ran to the back of the craft, including my friend's brother who was steering the boat, causing it to have a collision.

Life at Shirley Oaks was a fantastic experience. It taught me that a family is one of the most important things in your life, whether it is your direct family or people you live with as a family of friends. In Violet we each respected each other's different upbringing, religion and cultures. Basic 'ground rules' applied to every child in the house including the staff children who lived with us as a community. Generally no-one broke the rules because we valued our freedom. It taught us that rules are part of your life. If you break the rules then you must be prepared to face the consequences. I left Violet House at $16\frac{1}{2}$ because I had my daughter Katrina. I returned home to my parents until I got my own flat. My daughter Katrina is now 16. She is at college studying to be a social worker. She is awaiting her own flat and is extremely independent. My son Dean is eight. He is a very hyperactive but loving child. I work with people who advocate and support patients. I have complete backing from my family, friends, my children's fathers and their families. I am very lucky that I learnt from Shirley Oaks the value of help in all forms.

Description of Shirley Oaks

Shirley Oaks Children's Home lies 2½ miles east of central Croydon. Shirley Oaks main entrance sits on the right side near the base of a rise off Wickham Road, that leads into Upper Shirley roundabout.

The perimeter wall, built in four sections, is ornamented with stone spheres on top of each part, picked out in creamy white to contrast with the red brick wall. This frontage stretches about 290 feet, standing seven feet in height. Situated close to the foot of the wall and lying directly behind it is a corrugated bicycle shed. To the west is a row of poplar trees.

Visitors strolling down the narrow path (separated from the road by a kerb), to the right of Shirley Oaks Road, will first see to their left a house. This house has a three-pointed gabled roof, with a single bay window placed under the middle arch between two doors that provide access to the building.

Shirley Oaks' drive slopes gently downwards, almost unnoticed, soon after entering the grounds from the south. Continuing past a small wood, where the road turns slightly towards the left, one might imagine the Home to fall within a confined

The Orchard and view behind Heather and Holly Cottages

area. Once a couple of hundred yards inside the grounds, however, Shirley Oaks unfurls into a beautiful rural open estate, as grassy and leafy in parts as Shirley Hills that lie about a mile south of these attractive uneven lawns.

To the right there are more cottages. There is no obvious formation to the position of the buildings. These mainly twinned Edwardian residences are spaciously set apart from each other, yet seemingly turn their backs entirely on one another, across a sloping green expanse as though unaware of the other's existence.

As the journey further unfolds, it is evident that the individual cottages are named after trees, many of which can be found in the Home's grounds. They follow roughly in plural alphabetical and chronological order from the 'top', being the highest point of the Homes: Almond, Acacia/Ash, Aster, Beeches, Bramble/Birch. All the first floors of these buildings are decorated in pebble-dash.

When entering one of these cottages by the front door, you climb a few steps onto a small passage that leads into a corridor. To the

COTTAGES

First floor layout of double cottages

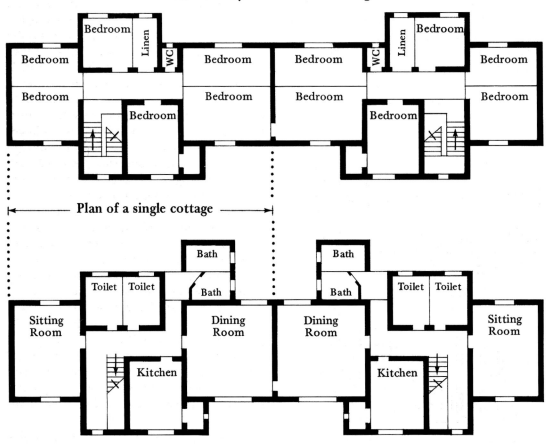

Plan of a single cottage

Ground floor layout

immediate right is a smart, bright teak staircase, complete with banisters and landing.

On the left is a sitting room. The ground floor has a set of washbasins and lavatories. The kitchen is small but inviting and has a stove. Adjoining the kitchen is a miniature hatch that looks out into a dining room, which is also used as a recreational area. To the immediate left is a glass window that peers over the main tail of a corridor and onto a narrow passage that leads past a set of black-painted coat-hangers. Then there is a drop in step where the passage passes a silver-finished shoerack to a set of bathrooms. Upstairs are four children's bedrooms, plain but comfortable, as well as two very small staff sleeping rooms. The red-stained polished floors, devoid of dust-collecting carpets, give an air of freshness to the place. The walls of these cottages have a cavity appearance.

Between the cottages of Bramble, Briar and Cherry, there is a loop road extending eastward, scooping past Cherry and Chestnut/

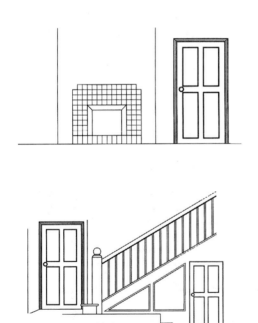

Daisy Cottages. Here, two narrow footpaths lead off from the main pathway beside the road. One lies along the front of the cottages, where a small garden plot is situated between the cottages and this path; the second runs behind the back of the buildings between the outhouses. All the cottages that lead off the Just beyond the twinned cottages of Briar/Cherry that stand across a sloping field are the administration offices, stores and accommodation for the superintendent. These buildings are about halfway down the length of Shirley Oaks Road. Further down the path are Thistle/Violet Cottages.

The road briefly finds a consistent plane before passing Elm/Fern, lifting slightly via Fir, gradually swaying past the nursery and Heather/Holly Cottages, before once again curving beyond an orchard. Facing this is the infirmary (originally Honeysuckle/Ivy) neatly enclosed by a low wooden fence. Virtually opposite the infirmary is Laburnam Cottage.

This part of the loop road is hemmed with low hedges that meet at a massive Edwardian water tower. The water tower is a landmark which can be seen from miles around, though strangely it appears somewhat detached from the site, looking over it, as if protecting it from enemies and intruders. The water tower holds 40,000 gallons of water. Around the tower are the swimming pool, laundry, carpenters, engineer's department, plumbers, tailors and shoe rooms. Two tinker boilers, one of which is on standby, provide steam for the swimming pool. The swimming pool has a white glazed wall, the bath itself is covered with terrazzo flooring. The pool measures seven yards by 13 yards, ranging from 3'6" to 4'6" deep.

Coming around to what was once the boys' side of the Home, there are more cottages. Larch, a single cottage, is almost opposite Laurel/Lavender on the left side of the road. A few yards in front, alternating across the road, are Lime/Linden and Maple/May Cottages. They are adequately dispersed, with plenty of green spaces and are well provided with trees.

The fields at the lowest level of Shirley, present immense problems when heavy rain and snow cause the drains to flood. Worst of all, they have two watercourses running underneath the grounds in front and behind Elm/Fern, straight across to the farm, which has poultry livestock and a small orchard, running either side of Musk/Myrtle Cottages to the other side of Shirley. The streams are open by the time they reach these two cottages and have a row of hedges along the far side. The land here is generally flat. Either side of Myrtle Cottage are two bridges where the stream flows. These bridges are constructed from furnace brick, probably recovered from furnaces or specifically purchased to support the erection of the bridges. These bridges may

have been built before the Home was established. The road rises slightly to Plane/Poplar, Primrose/Rose and Sycamore, another single cottage.

Beyond this second crossing lie Willow/Walnut and beyond them on the same side of the road is a single cottage, Yew. Then there is a pronounced dip in the road that creeps sharply to where the Home finally ends. In this part of the grounds Shirley County Primary School can be found. The school building is planned as a mixed department for boys and girls, and infants. There are 11 classrooms, with an attractive central hall that boasts a mini trio bable, either side of the roof, that rather dominates this single-storey building. Throughout the building are wood blocked floors.

The northern end of Shirley Oaks Road

View from behind Musk and Myrtle Cottages, 1983

meets Glenthorne Avenue, with access controlled by a double wooden gate. There is approximately a mile of road within the Homes.

When this cottage Home was first built, each abode would have had its own individual boundary. The numerous trees, coupled with picturesque setting and plenty of space, give the Home an open appearance.

Nowadays, there is little evidence that Shirley Oaks was once a Children's Home. Many of the open fields, trees and cottages that made Shirley so attractive are now a bygone memory. The cost of refurbishing and reordering of new networks of roads would be too astronomical. In fact, the Home has irreversibly changed.

The overwhelming impression that Shirley Oaks leaves is that of large open spaces between the cottages, with pockets of small

hedges scattered around 80 acres of land, with its varying angles of sloping landscape.

Perhaps it is something of a paradox that people are willing to pay large sums of money to reside on an estate and attend a hospital that had previously been a Home and school for underprivileged children.

However, not all of the past has gone. Those who spent many happy and sad years there have their own pictures, some of these may be summed up by the following rhyme that goes to the tune of 'Oh my Darling'.

"Come to Shirley, come to Shirley, come to Shirley
for a rest,
There's a notice at the entrance saying it's the
very best.
Don't believe it, don't believe it, for it's all a pack
of lies;
If it wasn't for the housewives we'd all be paralysed."

Cedar and Rowan Houses, 1983

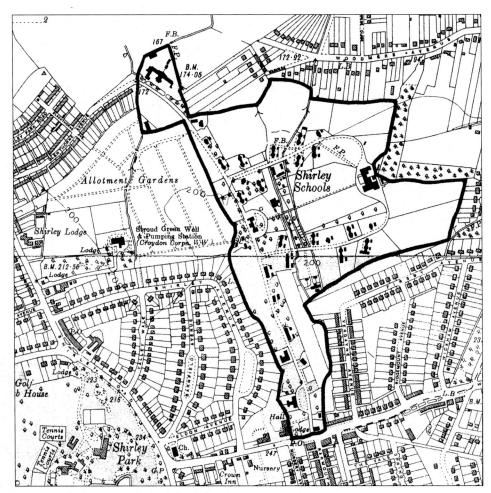

The Shirley site (outlined) is from an Ordnance Survey map of 1934

The Other London Village Homes

Six Homes were built by Poor Law Guardians towards the end of nineteenth century and the beginning of the twentieth and were transferred to the London County Council in 1930. Shirley Schools were run by the Bermondsey Union. The other Poor Law Unions adopted similar principles for the administration of their Homes.

Hornchurch

Initially Shoreditch Cottage Homes, Hornchurch Road, Hornchurch, Essex. Went over to LCC in 1930 and was renamed Hornchurch Children's Home. Later changed name to Saint Leonard's Children's Home, while managed by the London Borough of Tower Hamlets. It was closed in the mid 1980s.

Hornchurch, which went through three changes of name and closed in the mid-80s

Beechholme
Formerly Banstead District School, Banstead, Surrey. The oldest of the Residential Villages, it was opened in 1880 by the managers of the Kensington & Chelsea School District. Taken over by the LCC in 1930 and renamed Banstead Residential School. Administered by Wandsworth Council from 1965. Approx. 27 acres in size. Changed name to Beechholme in 1951 and closed in 1974.

Hutton Poplar
Hutton Residential School and Ongar Residential School (known as Hutton Poplar Training Schools, Hutton, Essex) were taken over by the LCC in 1930 and in 1932 they came under the same committee of management. Hutton was for children under 7 and over 11, and Ongar was for children 7–11 years old. From 1 April 1939 Ongar School became a special school, and children aged 7–11 went to Hutton. Family homes on the Aveley and Basildon Housing Estates were administered by the same committee.

Ashford Residential School
Ashford, Middlesex. Transferred to the LCC from West London School District in 1930; closed in 1955. The West London District must have survived the abolition of the districts, probably by continuing as a looser amalgamation of the Poor Law Union.

The Hollies
Opened on 30 October 1902 by the Greenwich and Deptford Board of Guardians. Originally called Sidcup Children's Home and later referred to as Sidcup Residential School. When LCC took over in 1930 it was renamed Lamorbey Residential School. Covered roughly 50 acres. It became The Hollies in 1950 and was officially closed in 1989.

The Hollies, which went through four changes of name between 1902 and 1989 on closure

The Shirley Schools in its picturesque setting c.1924. The Home remained almost unchanged until it was closed in 1983 and a new housing development changed the face of the landscape.

Further Reading

The following books can be found at the Reference Library of the London Metropolitan Archives.

STEWART, Susan, *The Central London District Schools 1855–1933: A Short History.* Hanwell Community (PP31)

CHANCE, W., MA, *Children under the Poor Law, their Education, Training and Aftercare.* Swan, Sonnenschein & Co Ltd, Paternoster Square, London

A Short History of the North Surrey District Schools

HITTON, J. P. (Intro), *The Boarding Out of Poor Law Children*

MONNINGTON, Walter, and LAMPARD, J., *Our London Poor Law School* (comprising descriptive sketches of these schools with map). Eyre and Spottiswoode, London

There is an annual reunion. For further information please contact:
Mrs Linda Cherry
37 Broomfield Road
Beckenham
Kent BR3 3QB
020 8650 4996